ALSO BY MARK FISHER

THE INSTANT
MILLIONAIRE

The
MILLIONAIRE'S SECRETS

⌇

Life
Lessons
in
Wisdom
and
Wealth

◆

MARK FISHER

A FIRESIDE BOOK
Published by Simon & Schuster

FIRESIDE
Rockefeller Center
1230 Avenue of the Americas
New York, NY 10020

First Fireside Edition 1997

FIRESIDE and colophon are registered
trademarks of Simon & Schuster Inc.

Designed by Amy Hill

Manufactured in the United States of America

3 5 7 9 10 8 6 4 2

Library of Congress Cataloging-in-Publication Data
Fisher, Mark
The millionaire's secrets : life lessons in wisdom and wealth/Mark Fisher.
p.   cm.
Sequel to: The instant millionaire.
1. Young men—New York (N.Y.)—Fiction.   2. Millionaires—Fiction.
3. Wealth—Fiction.   I. Title.
PS3556.I8142M55   1996
813',54—dc20   95-46841

ISBN 0-684-80281-3
0-684-80118-3 (Pbk)

To Nityananda

CONTENTS

Cʀʟʟ9

Contents

Contents

Contents

CHAPTER 1

*In which
the young man
feels estranged
at work . . .*

WHEN HE awoke in his modest, somewhat cluttered Brooklyn apartment, John Blake, a young man of thirty-two, short in stature but of a generally dynamic appearance, realized that it was already nine-thirty. He was late. Either his alarm clock hadn't gone off or he'd forgotten to set it.

There was no time for a shower, so he splashed his face with cold water, ran a comb through his hair, swallowed a vitamin C tablet, and then, feeling he'd need as much energy as possible to get through the day, took a second, and finally a third for good luck. He dressed as quickly as he could, in the same clothes he'd worn the night before, which he'd carelessly discarded on a chair; since his tie was still knotted around his shirt collar he just slipped the whole affair over his head like a sweater.

His old '65 convertible Mustang, which he cared for religiously, almost let him down for once, but after four or five tries it finally started. He thought, "It looks like this is going to be one of those days when I'll wish I hadn't gotten out of bed."

At the Gladstone Advertising Agency, which occupied an old but completely renovated building on Madison Avenue, and where he'd worked as a writer for the last few years, John's secretary, Louise, greeted him with a worried look.

"Where have you been? Gladstone is furious. He's been looking everywhere for you. The meeting is scheduled to start in five minutes, and he absolutely wanted to see you beforehand, along with Gate."

"Alarm clock trouble," John muttered as he disappeared into his office and began sorting through the pile of files on his desk. His secretary followed him in.

"The Cooper file, where is it?" John asked, turning his back to her.

"Right here," Louise replied, smiling calmly and handing him the file, which, with her usual efficiency, she had made sure to get ready.

"Thank you," he said, taking the large cardboard folder that contained the Cooper company logo, a photograph of a shoe that was to be promoted, and a picture of a man and a woman. "And I'll have a coffee, please, Louise," John added, lighting up a cigarette.

Cooper Shoes Incorporated had contracted the Gladstone Agency to do the publicity for a new men's shoe with a hidden heel that added three inches to the wearer's height. The picture, based on John's concept, depicted a very elegant—and very tall—woman walking along Fifth Avenue and winking at a man who had "grown" to a suitable height because of his Cooper shoes.

The only problem was that the text, due to be presented at that morning's meeting, and which John was supposed to have provided, was not written yet. He hadn't been able to think of a thing, and yet for years he'd been considered one of the agency's most brilliant writers.

He puffed nervously on his cigarette, trying to summon up the inspiration that rarely let him down. But his mind remained a total blank, almost as if he'd exhausted what was left of his creativity and imagination long ago. He consulted the notes he'd jotted down during the past week, pages and pages of text, titles, catchy headlines, dialogue. Nothing seemed to click. Tiny beads of sweat formed on his forehead. He had to come up with something, and fast. Very fast.

No sooner had Louise walked in the door with a

steaming hot cup of black coffee than his boss, Bill
Gladstone, followed by James Gate, strode into the office. Very short and completely bald, Gladstone possessed extraordinary energy, reflected in the almost
ferocious glitter of his minuscule blue eyes.

"Where were you, John? Do you realize what time it
is?" he snapped, tapping his watch. "You're pushing
your luck here, my boy. This is a three-hundred-thou-
sand-dollar account. The agency can't afford to lose it.
Nor can you," he added with thinly disguised menace.
"Now show me what you've got."

Before John could answer, his boss was leaning over
the file, staring at the picture of the man and woman.
Registering both surprise and alarm, he shouted,
"Where's my text? I don't understand. The meeting
starts in two minutes!"

"I'm still not sure," John said, holding up his notes.

Gladstone glanced warily at the notes, dozens of
pages darkened with John's neat script, and shouted,
"What do you expect me to do with that?"

James Gate, a remarkably handsome man with
bleached-blond hair and sky-blue eyes, and a whole
head taller than John, walked up and took a look at the
artwork, also noticing the missing text. Since he was
the one who had to make the presentation, he was un-
derstandably concerned, and turned pale.

"I don't know what's been happening to you the last few weeks, John, but you're just not the same."

"A few weeks . . ." John thought. It was more like a few months—a year, actually, maybe more.

For some time now he'd felt a terrible sense of foreboding, that if he waited too long it would be too late. He'd lose the power to dream, as had doubtless already happened to so many of his "dead" colleagues on the urban battlefield. All he really wanted to do was to open his own agency, or write a movie script, but he hadn't had the courage to follow through. He felt stifled and trapped.

"Come on, John, give me something here, get us out of this mess!" Gladstone shouted.

"What are we going to do?" Gate said.

"What about you? Don't you have any ideas?" his boss snapped.

Gate was not an idea man, and the thought of having to make his presentation with an incomplete layout literally terrified him.

"I don't know, we could say . . . uh . . ."

John wasn't listening to the two men. His old writer's reflexes were taking over, as he finally found what he was looking for. In his beautiful handwriting he carefully added a header to the artwork: "Only *he* knows that he's shorter. And when she finds out, it'll be too late, because they'll both be barefoot. . . ."

Gladstone read the text and burst out laughing. "Excellent!" he said. "Excellent!"

Gate read it and laughed, too, although his was a more subdued, almost polite laugh. He'd always envied John's brilliant mind but consoled himself with the thought that he earned twice as much money and was usually able to take all the credit for the company's successful campaigns.

"Let's hope the clients like it as much as you do," Gate said, still skeptical.

John didn't say anything, relieved that he'd been able to come up with a text that his boss found so wonderful under such extreme pressure, like the goose that laid the golden egg. At the same time he felt a little let down, aware that he could elicit his boss's approval—or disdain—simply by dropping a couple of lines of text on the table, text that he himself found trite, or in any case far from brilliant.

"Let's go," Gladstone said, picking up the artwork. "The clients are waiting in the boardroom."

John followed his boss and Gate to the conference room, where three representatives of the Cooper company, all in somber business suits, were chatting and sipping coffee.

Once the handshakes and introductions were over,

Gate, who had placed John's artwork on a large easel, lifted the cover, revealing the publicity campaign the agency had devised. He was a master at selling empty clichés, making them sound fresh and original, while appropriating other people's ideas, mostly John's, with disconcerting ease. John drank his coffee with mounting annoyance, a feeling that invariably took possession of him at meetings of this kind.

"Well, what do you think?" Gladstone said when Gate had finished.

The three clients put their heads together for a few seconds and spoke in lowered voices, creating a slight air of suspense. Then George Cooper said, "We're interested. We'll go ahead with it."

"Fine," Gladstone declared. "Welcome to the Gladstone family," he added, handing over two copies of a service contract that the clients signed on the spot.

Gladstone retrieved the agency's copy. The three men stood up and, after another polite exchange of handshakes, left the conference room. As soon as they were gone Gladstone turned to Gate, beaming with satisfaction, and the two of them did a high five.

"Another one in the bag, my dear vice president."

"Vice president?" Gate said, surprised, pretending not to understand.

"That's right, starting today, you're our new V.P."

"I'm honored, sir. Thank you."

Anyone else in John's shoes would certainly have felt some frustration. But he'd become insensitive to such outrage a long time ago.

Before leaving, Gladstone turned to John. "Oh, yes, John, I want to congratulate you, too. You see, I was right when I told you to make those changes. You did super work. Really great."

"Thanks," John said begrudgingly.

Gladstone was about to join Gate, waiting in the corridor, savoring his promotion, when he turned to John again and said, "Oh, and don't forget the Russian presentation Monday morning. It's a big deal, a seven-figure account. I don't know where those Russians are getting their money, but I have a feeling they're a lot less communistic than they used to be!" He laughed loudly, obviously proud of his little joke. "I want to see something really super, okay? You don't have anything planned for the weekend, I hope?"

"No, nothing," John said.

It happened every time. Since he wasn't married and had no family obligations, his boss took it for granted that he had nothing better to do on weekends—or on any night of the week, for that matter—than to put in hours and hours of overtime, working away with unlimited devotion, as if advertising were his only passion.

He felt like throwing a wrench into the works and quitting there and then. But he couldn't. He had nothing else lined up, and he didn't have a penny to fall back on. In fact, he was so deeply in debt he hadn't been able to use his overloaded credit cards for months.

The first thing John did after leaving the office that evening—in that morning's haste he'd completely forgotten—was to check the newspaper to see if he'd won the lottery. Since he hadn't, he threw away his tickets and bought two more, doing his best to concentrate while filling in the numbers, as if he thought he could exert some influence on his luck. Then he went home, with the voluminous Russian file under his arm, depressed at the prospect of having to work on it all weekend long.

For a few months now he'd been suffering from what could be called "weekend syndrome." During the week, overloaded as he was with work, he had no time to think about his life, the fact that he was still a bachelor at thirty-two, without a wife or children, or any social life to speak of, except for the people he came into contact with at the agency. But when the weekend rolled around he found himself face-to-face with the emptiness of his life, and it caused him anguish. The feeling—true or not—that he was leading an abnormal life tormented him. What he needed—

what he really needed—was a profound change.

For three nights running, in fact, he'd awakened from sleep with tears in his eyes, and each time he was able to remember the cause of his sadness. He had dreamed of a magnificent blue jay—his favorite bird as a child—with its wings amputated, and he had understood immediately that the wingless bird was none other than himself.

Not only did he find his solitude hard to bear, he couldn't explain it, either. Being a romantic despite a number of disappointing relationships, he still believed in love. Maybe he was too demanding, missing out on opportunities—the good times, as his father called them—because he didn't give the women who seemed interested in him (and there had been a number of these) enough of a chance.

Strangely enough, he always seemed to attract women who left him indifferent, while those he was attracted to hardly took any notice of him at all. It was as if the gods presiding over affairs of the human heart were amusing themselves by systematically thwarting his efforts.

One thing was certain, however, and that was that he preferred waiting for the "right" person rather than getting involved in stopgap—and therefore temporary—relationships that often left deep scars when they didn't work out, not to mention the fact that they were often a complete waste of time. In truth, he had started to lose faith in his quest for the woman with whom he wanted to spend the rest of his life. He felt as if he'd spent too much time, and used up too much hope, on his search already.

He realized that he just couldn't go on living the lonely life he'd been leading for years. The first thing he had to do was solve his money problems. But how? Who could help him? Certainly not his father, who earned just enough to make ends meet from the little bar he owned. Then who?

Suddenly, John remembered that he had a rich uncle, a man he hardly knew, really, generally seeing him only once a year at Christmas or on other rare occasions. He decided to pay him a visit. He could ask for advice—or better still, for money to help him quit his job and start his own agency, something he'd dreamed of doing for a long time. John picked up the phone and called him immediately to set up lunch for the following afternoon, then settled down to work on the sprawling Russian file.

The next day, his uncle gave him a very warm welcome but refused to give, or even lend, him any money. "I lend money only to rich people," he said jokingly, which tempered his refusal somewhat. Instead, he suggested that John meet a friend of his, an eccentric old millionaire who lived out on Long Island and who had helped him when he was just starting out. He even gave John a letter of recommendation.

CHAPTER 2

*In which
the young man
gets his first
real break . . .*

AROUND TEN o'clock the next morning John pulled up in front of the imposing gates of the millionaire's house, an immense Tudor-style mansion. A security guard asked him if he had an appointment. Instead of answering, John handed him the letter of recommendation his uncle had given him. The guard pressed a button, the gates swung open, and John drove his Mustang slowly through.

He parked, timidly climbed the thirty or so steps of an imposing outside stairway that was flanked by two ancient-looking stone lions, and rang the bell. He didn't have to wait very long before Henry, an old butler dressed in an impeccable uniform, opened the door. John explained the reason for his visit.

The butler informed John that his master was not available at the moment and suggested he wait in the garden, politely offering to escort him. John thanked him and followed him to an immense rose garden, where he noticed an old gardener,* in his seventies at least, leaning over a rosebush that he was carefully pruning, his face protected from the sun by a large yellow straw hat.

John stepped forward, and the man straightened up, interrupting his work. He smiled, and John was struck by his blue, extremely luminous eyes.

"What are you doing here?" the man asked in a melodious, slightly mocking voice.

"I came to see the instant millionaire."†

"For what reason, if I may ask?"

"Well, I just wanted some advice."

"I see. . . ."

The man resumed his pruning, seeming to lose interest in John, but stopped a moment later and said, "You wouldn't have ten dollars to lend me, would you?"

"Ten dollars? Well . . ." John dug into his pockets and pulled out all the bills and change he could find, a total of about fifteen dollars—he hadn't stopped at the bank

*Readers can find a detailed description of this encounter in *The Instant Millionaire*.

†This character first appeared in *The Instant Millionaire*.

to deposit his paycheck yet, and he was broke, as usual.

"Well, actually, this is all I have left."

"That's fine, it's more than I need," the gardener said with a triumphant smile. He took a step toward John, plucked a ten-dollar bill out of his hand, and stuffed it into his pocket. "What's ten dollars anyway? Who knows, tomorrow you might be a millionaire."

John didn't dare protest. After all, he was only a visitor to this prestigious mansion, and the one thing he didn't want to do was commit a blunder. But he couldn't help thinking that his visit, which was supposed to be enriching, hadn't started off very well at all, since it had already cost him ten dollars. It was clear that he didn't have a gift for holding on to money!

At that moment Henry, the butler, arrived and respectfully said to the gardener, "Sir, there is a slight problem. One of the cooks is leaving us today, and he absolutely insists we pay him what we owe him in cash. And, um . . . we're short ten dollars."

The gardener reached into his pocket and, to John's great surprise, pulled out an enormous roll of bills, all of large denominations—fifties, hundreds, and even a few thousands. With an ironic smile the old gardener took the ten-dollar bill he'd just borrowed from John and handed it to the butler, who bowed respectfully, turned on his heel, and walked away.

John was indignant. He felt cheated.

"Why did you ask me for ten dollars? You don't need it."

"Oh, but I do," the gardener replied. "Look," he said, skillfully spreading his roll of bills like a fan. "I don't have any ten-dollar bills. And I wasn't about to give him a hundred or a thousand!"

"You never know who you might be dealing with. . . ." John recalled the old maxim as a light flashed in his mind.

"You're the instant millionaire, aren't you?"

"That's what they call me."

"My name is John, John Blake," the young man said, offering his hand to the millionaire, who shook it after putting his billfold back into his pocket.

"I'm happy you came by, John," the older man said somewhat mysteriously, as if he'd been expecting the visit.

John thought it best not to question him further on the subject, and in any case he didn't have the chance to do so, as the eccentric millionaire said, "And what is it you want from me?"

"My uncle told me you could help make my dreams come true, help me become successful and make my fortune."

"I see. But tell me, how is it that you haven't already

made your fortune? Have you ever asked yourself that question?"

"No, not really."

"Well, maybe that's the first thing you should do. Go ahead, think out loud for me."

"I, uh . . ." John stammered, completely at a loss for words.

"I see," the millionaire said. "You're not used to thinking out loud. Or maybe you're not used to thinking at all. Well, listen, may I invite you for lunch? It might give you the strength you need to think clearly."

John accepted with relief, and the two men soon found themselves seated in an immense dining room at a table large enough for thirty guests. Two walls of the dining room were equipped with very high stone fireplaces, both lit up with crackling fires. John had never seen a dining room like it, nor so sumptuous a table.

As he dug into his salmon steak and salad, the millionaire questioned John.

"Do you like what you're doing?"

"Yes. Well, actually, no. I work for an ad agency. But I'd like to have my own agency."

"Do you really think, deep down, that you could be successful in that area?"

"Yes."

"Well, what's the problem?"

"The problem is I don't have any money to get started."

"When I started out I didn't have any money, either," said the old man, glancing around him, "and I must say I haven't done too badly."

"But without money, I really don't see how—"

"Your real problem is fear. You don't have enough confidence in yourself. If you had faith, real faith, you'd succeed. Do you know that anything a man can conceive of, anything he can believe in, he can also accomplish?"

The millionaire reached into his pocket and pulled out a coin. Absently tossing it for heads or tails, he asked John, "Tell me, how much would you be willing to pay to learn the secret of success?"

"I don't have a cent."

"If you had money."

"I don't know, a hundred dollars. . . ."

The millionaire laughed, following the coin's trajectory through the air with his eyes. "A hundred dollars! My Lord, we've got some work to do. Give me another figure."

"A thousand dollars."

Once again the old man burst out laughing. "If you really believed there was a secret, you'd offer me a whole lot more than that. Go on, try again. If you had money, how much would you be willing to offer me for the secret?"

"I don't know, let's say twenty-five thousand."

"Good, that's very good. It's not a lot, but at least you're making progress."

The two men talked for a few hours, sometimes walking through the rose garden, sometimes seated, drinking tea, and the millionaire revealed to John the secret that had allowed him to amass his prodigious fortune. John was amazed at how simple it was. Why hadn't he thought of it? Perhaps because he'd never stopped to consider. Or maybe because he didn't believe a secret existed.

By the end of their long conversation the millionaire had gotten to know John a lot better, and found he liked him: a man who was that brilliant, and yet who had had such bad luck up to then, merited a little helping hand from destiny. He reached into his pocket, pulled out his roll of bills, and said, "Here."

John didn't quite understand at first.

"You're . . . ?"

"Yes, I'm giving it to you. There's twenty-five thousand dollars there, give or take a couple of hundred. My pocket money."

"Twenty-five thousand dollars? You're giving me twenty-five thousand dollars?"

"Well, actually I'm not giving it to you, I'm lending it to you. One day, five, ten years from now, when you're rich, you'll help someone else get started, in the same way that I'm helping you today. Thus the chain will be completed, and what must be accomplished shall be accomplished."

He paused for a moment, then added, "All my life people have thought of me as a successful businessman. I, on the other hand, have never considered myself anything more than a simple gardener. If I amassed a colossal fortune, it was only to show people of little faith the power of the mind. Whenever you can, concentrate on the heart of the rose. One day you will understand what I'm trying to tell you."

After handing over the surprising legacy, the old millionaire moved closer to John and, with his right index finger, touched his forehead between the eyes, saying, "Discover who you really are. Truth will set you free."

Then he left him alone. John felt as if he'd just lived through one of the most important moments of his life, not only because of the incredible sum of money he'd just been given but because there was something magical about his meeting the old millionaire.

Just then Henry entered the dining room and asked John if he'd like to freshen up before leaving. John ac-

cepted, realizing that his strange visit to the millionaire's house was coming to an end. He followed the butler upstairs. Henry stopped at the door to one of the
numerous rooms and handed John an envelope, a very
large envelope made of exquisite paper and bearing a
red wax seal in the form of a rose.

"This is from my master," the butler explained.

When John opened it, alone in his room, he realized
with emotion that the envelope contained the spiritual
testament of the old millionaire, a document about
sixty pages long. He leafed through it and then, ready
to leave, decided he'd better thank his host for all he'd
done for him.

He went back down to the dining room, walked
through the luxurious living room, but didn't see the
millionaire and thought he might have gone back to
the garden. He was not mistaken. But when he got
there an incredible surprise awaited him. The old man
was stretched out in the middle of a pathway, his face
perfectly serene, hands crossed on his chest like someone laid to rest in a tomb, holding a rose.

Overcome with grief, John concluded that the old
man was no longer of this world, which was why he had
given him his spiritual testament, and the sum of
money, a few minutes before.

But how had the old man been able to predict his

death? A mystery that would have to go unanswered. The man had been amazing. . . .

After a few seconds had passed, John stepped forward, intending to take the rose as a kind of souvenir of their meeting, but then changed his mind. The flower belonged to the millionaire and would be his final companion.

CHAPTER 3

*In which
the young man
regains his
wings . . .*

THE FOLLOWING Monday in the Gladstone agency's large conference room the president of the Russian company, visibly disappointed by James Gate's shabby, completely unimaginative presentation, rose from his chair. His acolytes immediately followed suit.

"I think we'll take a look at another agency," the president declared. "This isn't what we had in mind."

Gladstone, devastated, didn't even bother to protest. Without John, who was nowhere to be found on this Monday morning, neither he nor James Gate, his new vice president, had been able to make the grade. When the Russians had gone, Gladstone's face—actually, his entire bald skull—grew purple with rage as he turned savagely on Gate.

"Are you a complete idiot or what? Couldn't you come up with anything better than that? You could have talked about marketing, about strategy. . . . You're supposed to be an M.B.A., aren't you?"

"Yes, but, I mean . . . having to improvise like that . . . There was no way I could guess what Blake had in mind, was there?"

"Listen, an M.B.A. is supposed to be able to handle any kind of situation, even an emergency. And as for your promotion, I'm putting that on ice until further notice. A vice president who doesn't know what to do when the shit starts flying isn't worth a damn."

"But, Mr. Gladstone, you can't do that."

"Yes, I can, and the proof is that I just did it. And now, if you'll excuse me, there's something I want to say to that little jerk Blake. He'll find out who calls the shots around here, wait and see."

John had arrived at the agency just a few minutes before, surprising everyone both by appearing totally unconcerned about his late entrance and by distributing roses to all the secretaries. No one had ever seen him look so confident, so charming, so easygoing, completely unlike the harried, overworked shadow of a man he'd been for over a year now.

His secretary accepted the last of the roses with a mixture of surprise and anxiety.

"Oh, Mr. Blake, where have you been? You should have called me! Mr. Gladstone's going to kill you."

"Ah!" was all John said. Without further comment he began gathering up his personal effects and piling them in a cardboard box. Gladstone strode into the office in a rage.

"Where the hell have you been, Blake? Do you realize what you've done? We just lost the Russian contract because of you!"

"Wasn't Gate there?"

"Yes, but he's an idiot. Now, will you give me the pleasure of answering my question immediately? This makes two mornings in a row that you're late. You're really starting to piss me off."

John looked at him with an amused smile and said, "Sure it's not your prostate?"

It was well known at the agency that Gladstone, living in a permanent state of stress, had developed gland problems of a personal nature. A number of jokes had been circulated on the subject.

"My prostate has nothing to do with this. You're the one who's going to have problems, I can promise you that. Do you know that I can fire you for what you just did?"

"No, you can't."

"What do you mean I can't?" Gladstone shouted.

"You can't fire me, because I'm resigning."

"You're resigning?" Gladstone sputtered in disbelief.

"Yes, effective . . ." John paused to consult his watch. "Effective at eleven thirty-seven."

Bill Gladstone was not used to people resigning. He was more used to firing people, occasionally taking a savage delight in doing so. First he thought it was a joke. Who would dare resign from the Gladstone Agency, in his opinion the best agency in the world?

John turned his back on his boss and continued gathering up the few sad ornaments that decorated his desk and placing them in the cardboard box. Gladstone felt a momentary urge to physically attack him but regained control, thinking rapidly.

"Listen, John, I'd like you to think about this. I think you may be acting a little hastily here. I'm ready to wipe the slate clean about the Russian thing. We can sit down and talk things over. That raise I promised you, well, I'm not the kind of man who doesn't keep a promise. Starting next month you're getting another five percent. . . ."

John turned around, frowning, examining a miniature horse he held in his hand. Instead of replying, as if Gladstone hadn't said anything since he walked in, John asked, "Do you like this statue? I don't think I want to keep it."

In a paroxysm of rage, Gladstone seized the statue and hurled it against the wall, smashing it to bits. It wasn't often that anyone made fun of him, especially not a common little employee.

"You got a better offer somewhere else?" Gladstone demanded. "That's it, isn't it?"

"No," John replied.

"Listen," Gladstone said, his voice taking on a paternal tone, "you're one of our best people, you have enormous talent. That's why I'm ready to break policy concerning salaries and offer you a thousand more."

"A thousand?"

"Per month, of course. That makes twelve thousand a year."

"Twelve thousand more a year," John reflected, "that's strange. Less than twenty-four hours ago I started thinking I was worth more than I was getting, and now my boss is offering me twelve thousand more a year."

"Well?" Gladstone said impatiently.

"Twelve thousand . . ."

"Oh, and of course you get a company car."

John couldn't believe it. This was something to think about. It was also the last thing he'd expected to happen. He hesitated. The raise he was being offered was enormous. Twelve thousand! And a car on top of that! Shouldn't he accept? With the twenty-five thousand he already had he could pay off all his debts, clean the slate. But if he accepted wouldn't he be betraying the old millionaire's trust? And wouldn't it also mean burying his dreams for good, renouncing what he really was—and especially what he wanted to become—once and for all? He realized that a raise and a new car wouldn't solve anything.

"Thanks, but . . . it's not a question of money," he finally replied.

"You want to start up on your own, don't you?" Gladstone sneered. "Well, let me tell you something, you haven't got what it takes! You'll fall flat on your face! You have absolutely no talent, and I'm going to see to it that your name is dirt in every agency in town!"

John looked at the sorry collection of items in the cardboard box and decided he didn't want any of it. He'd rather make a clean break and leave everything behind, just forget about this not-so-glorious period of his life. As he walked out of the office he shoved the box into Gladstone's arms.

Once he was out on the sidewalk, John experienced a feeling of extraordinary freedom. He'd been dreaming of quitting for so long, and now he'd finally done it. He was overcome by a strange sense of exaltation, something like what he'd felt when, as a boy, the first day of summer holidays would arrive and school would shut its doors for two months. He felt that the future belonged to him and that, finally, he was embarking on a new life.

CHAPTER 4

*In which
the young man
experiences
failure . . .*

"I'M SO sorry, Mr. Blake, but we already have an ad agency."

John, who these days usually looked rather cheerful, hung up with a frown. This was the tenth refusal that day. If it had been his first week on the job it wouldn't have seemed so bad, but it had been six months since he'd opened his own agency. Inspired by the instant millionaire, John was full of confidence in the future and convinced that he would quickly succeed.

But all he'd been able to dig up—aside from one contract that had brought in five thousand dollars—was a series of piddling little jobs that paid hardly anything. All the big companies—and even the little ones—that he'd approached had told him the same thing: "We don't know anything about your agency" or, "You haven't got any experience" or, "Who are your other clients?" or, "We always work with the larger agencies." In other words, "Don't call us, we'll call you."

And yet when he'd started he thought he had everything he needed to make a go of it. He had a number of years of experience at a prestigious agency under his belt. He was an award-winning writer, never at a loss for original ideas, capable of meeting the toughest deadlines—a "must" in the field of advertising, where everyone expects to have things done "by yesterday." John had an excellent reputation among his previous clients, and he was confident that his charm would help out, too.

In order to devote as much time as possible to creative work and the quest for new clients, John had hired an assistant as soon as he opened his agency. Her name was Rachel Winter. What struck him when he chose her from among the other candidates who had responded to his Help Wanted ad was the openness and warmth of her smile. She seemed to believe in him right from the start, and that touched him, all the more so since a couple of other candidates had actually turned around and left when they saw the tiny office John was proposing they work in.

And even though, when he hired her, he had firmly

resolved not to mix work with feelings, he could not help falling in love with her. Her long chestnut hair, naturally curly, with touches of gold, and her large green eyes, shining with both intelligence and gentleness, dissolved any reticence he might have initially harbored. In time, Rachel developed the same feelings even though, like John, she'd sworn never to get involved with someone she was working with, especially her boss. But right from the start she felt that she meant more to him than a simple employee—she was his assistant, and in a sense his partner.

Unfortunately, John's business affairs weren't really getting off the ground. He'd already spent half the capital he had when he started and was seriously wondering if it hadn't been a mistake to quit his job so hastily.

He also wondered if his father, who had died a few months earlier, hadn't been right in saying that he wasn't made for wealth or a life in the fast lane. Maybe his mistake, his big mistake, had been not taking over his father's little bar instead of opening an ad agency.

Just as John was replaying in his mind all of his plans and wondering where he was going wrong, Rachel walked in, looking preoccupied.

"I'm leaving," she said with seriousness.

"It's only four o'clock," John replied, glancing down at his watch. "I . . ."

"I know, but it's quiet, and I . . . I'm leaving for a few days, John. I think we both need a little time apart. I feel as if I've become a burden to you. . . . I know things aren't going well at the agency, and your self-doubts are having an effect on us, since we work together. I'm going to spend a few days with a friend in Boston." Rachel paused, then added, "I'll call you when I get back."

Although John was annoyed, he didn't try to talk her out of it. He was aware that a kind of tension had begun to develop between them. And although her unexpected announcement worried John, maybe a few days apart would be a blessing. He could rethink his plans for the agency. Just as he thought this, John noticed that Rachel grew pale and lifted a hand to her forehead.

"What's the matter, don't you feel well?" John asked.

"No, it's nothing, I'm just a little dizzy."

He poured her a glass of water and she drank it down. Then, with a sad smile, she left, without even kissing him, as if she suddenly had something important to take care of. Her hurried departure and the little oversight about not kissing him good-bye sent a twinge through John's heart.

Panic hit him. Why hadn't he tried to make her stay? Didn't he realize that he might be losing her? That if he waited it might be too late? How could he be sure that this little trip, this temporary separation, wasn't just a pretext, a way of preparing him for a permanent end to their relationship? But he was so preoccupied with the way things were going at the agency, so concerned about the prospect of imminent failure, that he waited a little too long before he got up and went after her, so that by the time he reached the corridor, intending to ask for an explanation—and, even more important, for some kind of reassurance that nothing had changed between them—the doors of the elevator had closed behind her and she was gone. Sadly, John returned to his office, where he reflected long and hard on his situation.

His thoughts brought him back to his lack of success. Everything had seemed so easy in the beginning. A few months ago, after meeting the old millionaire, he had felt that the world belonged to him and that all he had to do was apply a few simple rules to achieve success. John felt that he possessed some form of greatness, some talent as yet unexpressed, but then why hadn't he succeeded? Maybe he'd misunderstood the millionaire's instructions.

Chapter 5

In which
the young man
meets a remarkable
beggar . . .

The next morning John woke up later than usual. He had slept badly, disturbed by all kinds of strange dreams. He went to his office, intending to get some work done, but his heart wasn't in it. Rachel wasn't around, and on top of that it was a holiday, so nothing much was likely to happen.

He felt he couldn't stay inside and decided to take a stroll around the city. He walked for a good half hour, enjoying the beautiful weather. When he got to Times Square, a very old beggar in a threadbare navy blue coat, his face partly covered by a black brimmed hat, approached him.

"Would you have ten dollars you could give me?"

"Ten dollars!" John said, not without some animosity, surprised by the beggar's audacity. "No, I don't even have a dollar on me."

The beggar lifted his head. As he turned to walk away he handed John a single rose, and with a disarming smile he said, "For luck. Sorry to bother you. I wish you an excellent day."

This was uttered with complete sincerity, as if he'd known John for years.

John looked at the rose in his hand and hoped it would strengthen his resolve and break his spell of bad luck as the beggar promised. The flower's mysterious beauty fascinated him. He saw it as a subtle, perfect symbol of success, which could be achieved only by confronting the danger represented by its thorns. Suddenly he recalled one of the last things the old millionaire had said to him. "Concentrate on the heart of the rose. . . . Concentrate on the heart of the rose." He could still hear the old man's voice when the remarkable kindness expressed by the beggar struck him. A few months ago a complete stranger had given him twenty-five thousand dollars. Had he become so miserly, so stingy, that he couldn't even give a beggar a few pennies?

But it wasn't only that, it wasn't only the man's voice and affability that had disturbed him. More than anything it was the man's unique eyes, shining with such extraordinary brightness, although he'd only seen them for a fraction of a second when the beggar had lifted his head.

His eyes seemed to reveal some higher ideal, some sense of incomparable nobility. John felt troubled by the thought that he knew that gaze, that he'd seen those eyes somewhere before.

A shiver ran through his whole body as he recalled who the eyes reminded him of: the old millionaire. No less disturbing was the fact that the beggar had asked for exactly the same amount of money as the millionaire, whom John had mistaken for a gardener earlier: ten dollars! He couldn't quite bring himself to believe it was just a coincidence.

But it was impossible: he'd seen the old man's dead body right there in the rose garden. On the other hand, maybe he hadn't really been dead. John pictured the old man stretched out on the pathway in the garden with a rose placed on his breast. Come to think of it, he'd looked very much alive, even in his state of eternal rest. Yet how could a man, even one as amazing as the old millionaire, return from the realm of the dead?

John thought that, dead or not, a man as rich as the millionaire would never dress like a vagabond. But then a mysterious voice—maybe the child inside him—said that, yes, it was possible. As he rushed forward, intending to catch up to the old beggar, who was jauntily making his way through the crowd, he collided with a passerby, an obese elderly woman who dropped her bag of groceries on the sidewalk.

Despite his haste, John made sure the woman was all right and helped her pick up her scattered groceries. This done, he looked around, only to find that the beggar had disappeared.

In a panic he started running. After a few strides he thought he saw him, turning the corner onto Broadway. John ran faster. As he rounded the corner he saw the old man standing in front of a shop window, staring at some cakes. His heart beating with joy, John hurried over and touched the man respectfully on the shoulder. The beggar turned around, but it wasn't the same one who had asked for the ten dollars. In his haste John hadn't even noticed that this man wasn't wearing a hat—it was just his dark overcoat that looked the same.

Disappointed, John apologized and then surprised the beggar by giving him ten dollars. The man, thinking it was some kind of scam, looked around to see if John didn't have an accomplice hiding in the shadows, ready to jump him and steal what little money he had. But he saw no one and, reassured, thanked his benefactor and hurried into the pastry shop.

John hurried back to Times Square, hoping there

was still a chance he'd find the mendicant he was looking for. He looked everywhere, but without any luck.
Although his suspicions that the tramp was none other
than the old millionaire come back to life were completely unrealistic, John couldn't help feeling a little depressed. Even an absurd hope can sometimes be
comforting.

He hung around Times Square for a while, then set
off on one of the side streets heading across town. His
emotional state had made him thirsty, and he decided
to stop somewhere and have a drink. He recognized a
coffeehouse he'd been to before and headed for its sidewalk terrace. He was about twenty feet away when he
saw the old beggar.

At first he thought he was dreaming. And yet no,
there he was, seated at a table with an enormous glass
of orange juice in front of him, wearing the same
shabby clothes—a somber old coat and a large black
hat—nonchalantly tossing a coin in the air to see if it
landed heads or tails, exactly as the old millionaire had
done during their lunch together. On one throw he
tossed the coin too high and missed when he tried to
catch it. He watched it roll along the sidewalk toward
John, who quickly bent down and picked it up.

As he straightened up he met the old man's gaze
and was once again overcome with emotion. His intu-

ition had been right. This beggar with the extraordinary eyes, sparkling with life and joy, was none other than the old millionaire. When he realized that John had finally recognized him, the millionaire broke into a smile that expressed worlds of wisdom. Unlike John, he didn't seem in the least surprised to be meeting again this way, completely by "chance," on a New York street. After all, hadn't he predicted—or rather, orchestrated—the encounter?

Still experiencing the aftershocks of his utter astonishment, John, coin in hand, walked over to the old millionaire and asked a question he knew sounded completely absurd.

"How come you're not dead?"

"Because I'm alive," the millionaire replied, his smile broadening

"But I don't understand! It's impossible! You were on the ground in your garden. I saw you."

"As Shakespeare said, there's a lot more to the world than can be found in philosophy books. I was simply in a state of deep sleep, getting back in touch with my real self. That's a nice tie you're wearing," he added.

Surprised by the unexpected compliment, John raised a hand to his tie, wondering if it was just another coincidence or if the old millionaire, endowed with some mysterious power of perception, had guessed what sentimental value the tie held for him, having once be-longed to his father.

"Thanks," he said, looking embarrassed.

John didn't ask any more questions about the eccen-tric millionaire's "resurrection," although it did seem very strange and inexplicable.

There was a strained silence. Touching his tie, John began to think about all the frustration of the last few months, the repeated failures he'd encountered. More than once he'd doubted the value of the millionaire's advice. He felt a wave of resentment rising inside him, threw the coin on the table, and declared, "Because of you I quit my job. And now I'm on the verge of bank-ruptcy."

The old man looked at the coin with some surprise, as if John's veiled accusation troubled him deeply. Then he smiled again and replied, "If all I'd done was given you a fish to eat instead of trying to teach you how to be a fisherman, you'd have something to reproach me for. But not only did I reveal all the secrets of wealth to you, I also gave you quite a large fish, one worth twenty-five thousand dollars, as you may recall."

Just as he said that, a black limousine stopped next to them and a chauffeur stepped out. John didn't take long to realize that not only did the old man know him, but that he was *his* chauffeur, Edgar.

Chapter 6

*In which
the millionaire
teaches the young man
how to think like a
millionaire . . .*

❖

THE MILLIONAIRE greeted the chauffeur with a smile and asked him to open the trunk of the limousine. The old man extracted an ancient wooden box, intricately carved, and then invited John to take a ride in his limo. The three men drove off.

At a red light the old man lowered his window and pointed to a man standing on the curb wearing a very badly fitting suit, the pants much too short, and holding a battered briefcase. He asked John the following question: "Do you know what makes that fellow different from me?"

"Well, he doesn't have a chauffeur, he probably doesn't have your bank account, and he'd never dare dress like a tramp."

The millionaire burst out laughing. John certainly had a sense of humor.

"True enough, true enough. But the biggest difference, the fundamental difference, lies in this box," the old man said, referring to the wooden box on his knees. "This box was given to me by my master when I was just starting out and is one of the main reasons for my success. And now I'm giving it to you, since I don't need it anymore. One day, when the time has come, you'll pass it on to another man or woman, so that the chain is not broken and the teaching is transmitted."

John looked curiously at the beautiful ancient box, impatient to open it. What could be inside? Precious jewels? Title to some property or some huge bank account? A secret formula? An infallible plan for making a fortune? The old man handed John the box with an ephemeral smile. John quickly opened the box and was unable to hide his disappointment when all he found inside was an old radio. The thing must have been at least forty years old, if not more. John lifted it out of the box and regarded the millionaire skeptically.

"That fellow," said the old man, referring to the ill-dressed man on the curb, waiting for his bus, "is, with all due respect, very much like a savage living in the forest who has never seen a radio."

The light changed to green and the limo drove on.

"Imagine finding a primitive savage in the middle of the jungle. You show him this radio and tell him that sounds can come out of the box. And not only sounds but human voices and music. He'd probably think you were insane. The existence of radio waves, being invisible, would be completely beyond his range of understanding.

"Ordinary people resemble this savage. They don't believe that ideas are real, just as the savage doesn't believe radio waves are real. And yet we know radio waves exist, even though we can't see them. Unfortunately, most ordinary people's education goes no further than that. It ends exactly where the education of extraordinary persons begins. Extraordinary people know that ideas are very real entities, that every idea we emit tends to concretize, attracting the people and circumstances that can help make it a reality. And it doesn't matter if the idea is positive or negative. Extraordinary people know that ideas are real things. They know that the brain, the mind, is like this radio, that it can produce extraordinarily beautiful music, that it contains enough wealth to satisfy their needs for the rest of their lives. And I'm not just talking about money, I'm talking about accomplishment. If the man we saw a moment ago were able to use his inner powers, he could make his dreams come true and become a more fully realized version of himself. Take a real millionaire, take away everything he has, and put him in that man's situation. In a few months, a few years at most, he will have rebuilt his fortune. Why? Because the most important thing he has could not be taken away from him—his mind."

The old man paused for a moment and then continued. "Once you've come up with an initial list of ideas, you have to establish your priorities. Ask yourself the following question: 'If I had the time to work on only one of the ideas that sprang into my mind, which one would I choose? Which one seems to have the most potential?' Once you've answered that question, concentrate all your efforts on making that idea a reality."

"But," said John, "how can I know if the idea I choose is the right one? I know lots of people who thought they had a brilliant idea and whose lives were ruined because of it."

"You have to rely on your inner wisdom, on your intuition."

"But how do I know that my intuition isn't wrong?"

"Good point," the millionaire said, smiling. "I see that you're learning more and more how to think, how to ask the right questions. It is absolutely essential that you program your mind correctly, in a positive way, by repeating formulations like the one I already mentioned to you—*'Day by day, in every way, I am getting better and better'*—out loud, every morning. Don't forget that there's a dark side to the mind as well, a side that can be extremely malicious. Millions of people are controlled by this dark power without even being aware of it. That is precisely where the power of darkness lies, in its ability to hide its real nature—and especially its destructive influence."

"I see," said John.

"This principle of setting up priorities can be applied to any area of your life. Ask yourself which, out of all your activities, are most important to you, which ones bring you the greatest happiness. If you think about it, you'll understand that everything we do has only one objective—bringing us closer to our real self, to our spiritual self-realization. When you understand that, you'll be able to dedicate yourself completely, without any fooling around, without wasting even a minute of your time, because you'll understand that you've already wasted years, centuries even. You'll stop wasting time because everything you do will bring you closer to that unique and exalted point where the real voyage begins, the voyage you've been preparing yourself for throughout all your past lives.

"People's biggest mistake is thinking they have all the time in the world to do what is important. The really great sages and entrepreneurs of this world live each day as if it were their last, continually dedicating themselves to the essential tasks. Think about it."

The limousine was negotiating through traffic along one of New York's busier thoroughfares on its way to the millionaire's Long Island residence.

"Most people live in a kind of permanent stupor. They keep hoping, in a vague sort of way, that something will happen to improve their lives, some event, some chance encounter, a lucky lottery number or a change in government policy. They don't realize that everything begins and ends with themselves, that they and they alone are responsible for their destiny. The ideas that dominate their minds will eventually direct their lives. What we are inside will always eventually become apparent on the outside. Everything the human mind conceives of and believes in can be accomplished. Whenever you forget this great principle, whenever you doubt its veracity, just open this box and look at the old radio."

As he meditated on the old man's words, John put the radio back into the box and closed the lid. The two men remained silent for the rest of the journey, which lasted another half hour. John felt good, calmer than he'd been for days, weeks even, as if he were finally coming home after a long and arduous voyage. He realized that the millionaire had become a kind of spiritual father to him and that finding him again had helped him forget, albeit temporarily, his business troubles.

It is true that the old man possessed a unique quality, proper to all great souls, of being able to affect others without talking, simply through the energy emitted by his person, by radiating his own inner joy and light.

CHAPTER 7

*In which
the young man
discovers that he can
be both the gardener
and the rose at the
same time . . .*

◈

THEY WERE now driving past the sumptuous houses of the Hamptons, and the limousine soon came to a stop in front of an imposing set of gates. The chauffeur Edgar used a remote control device to open them. Then, after winding their way up a drive bordered by flowers of all kinds, they saw a vast building come into view.

John thought it was the millionaire's new house. But on closer inspection he realized that this was just the garage, with no less than six sets of double doors. When he finally saw the house a few seconds later he was a little disappointed. It was much less grand than the millionaire's previous Tudor-style mansion. But he soon realized his mistake as they moved closer to the house, which had a good twenty rooms spread over three floors, with three stone chimneys, and he saw a sign reading "EDGAR'S RESIDENCE."

"Edgar," thought John, "Edgar the chauffeur . . . this is his house!"

They headed past the chauffeur's residence and through a small but very dense wood that gave onto a meadow, where a number of horses pranced freely or grazed at their leisure and one young colt sucked on its mother's teat.

John admired the horses a moment and then saw a magnificent building, three times as large as Edgar's, ahead of them. It was constructed in the same style but had more floors and looked much more luxurious, surrounded with fountains, statues, trees, and flower beds.

"The guest house," the old millionaire said. "But if you have no objection, you can spend the night in the main residence."

They arrived, finally, and this time John understood what the word *wealth* really meant. It took his breath away. The house was a reproduction of a seventeenth-century French castle. It had four stories, five or six towers, and at least fifty windows.

"Here we are," the old man said.

John couldn't help thinking that the old millionaire must be much richer than he thought, since a castle like this was worth at least thirty million dollars, maybe more, especially since it stood on such an immense strip of land in Southampton, where real estate cost a fortune.

A butler and maid were there to greet the owner of the estate. They seemed to have great respect for him, which was normal for members of a household staff—but more than that, they both seemed to love him like a real father.

It must be said that the old millionaire was neither authoritarian nor condescending with any of his servants but seemed to treat them like his own children. It occurred to John that no one would ever dream of laughing at him, even if he happened to be wearing the strangest clothes.

The millionaire handed his black hat to the butler, telling him to treat it with the greatest care, and instructed the maid to prepare a room for his guest, the best room in the house, if you please. As he did so he turned and looked at John, as if to assure himself that he wasn't being too forward in assuming that he would want to spend the night. John simply nodded his head as a way of saying that he accepted the invitation with pleasure.

"If you like I can show you my new rose garden before we visit the rest of the house," the millionaire suggested.

"I'd love to see it," John replied.

They left Edgar and the other servants and walked slowly around the castle, complete with waterfalls and fountains, past an immense swimming pool of irregular shape.

The garden was protected by a very tall, perfectly pruned cedar hedge. Near the entrance John noticed a solar clock and a bronze plaque, green with age, inset with a curious saying: "In the heart of the rose lies the secret of all things."

The millionaire walked on ahead of John. The garden, crisscrossed by a number of pathways, must have been two hundred yards long and about a hundred yards wide, and contained every type of rose imaginable. The far end of the garden sloped down to the sea, shining and beautiful, with a few sailboats skimming along in the steady breeze.

"This is really an incredible place," John said. He was sincerely moved by the beauty of the rose garden, the largest he'd ever seen in his life.

One rosebush at the entrance of the garden stood out from all the rest. While the others were remarkably vigorous and bushy, this one was stunted, all dried out—almost dead, in fact. The millionaire stopped and examined one of its branches, which showed no sign of parasites, aphids, and so on. Bending over, he examined the base of the bush and noticed a few buds and three or four tender little leaves. His face lit up with a sad smile. Straightening up, he said, "I came back here just to take care of this rosebush. Afterward I'll be leaving again. My work here will be finished."

And he turned and walked on without giving John a chance to question this rather mysterious statement. John watched him walking down the pathway, admiring the old man's almost majestic bearing, despite the shabbiness of the coat he was wearing.

Perhaps it was the glorious scent of the multitude of roses, or the wind coming off the sea, but since he'd entered the rose garden it seemed to John that his mind had grown suddenly calm, as if it had slowed down, leaving more "space" between his thoughts. He felt free of cares, happier than he could remember being for years, since way back in early childhood.

For a few seconds he even seemed to forget where he was, and even who he was. He emerged from this all too brief moment of serenity feeling unexpectedly refreshed, a rare occurrence for him, and wondered what his life would be like if he could enter a similar state of mind whenever he wanted to.

He quickened his pace and caught up with the millionaire, who was ambling along in a leisurely fashion, almost floating above the ground, quite astonishing for a man of his years. They soon reached a pond in the middle of the garden, dotted with water lilies bearing beautiful yellow flowers. A few white ducks were frolicking about joyously, while a majestic solitary black swan looked on, apparently refusing to have anything to do with them.

A strange metallic sphere constructed of eight separate bands, and mounted on a sturdy pole, dominated the center of the pond. At first John thought it was some kind of weather vane, but then decided its function was purely decorative. Perhaps the occasional bird used it as a perch.

The millionaire stopped before a rosebush, bent forward, and breathed in its perfume. He stayed like that for a long moment, absorbed in his olfactory contemplation. John didn't dare interrupt him—there was something almost religious about the gesture. After a few seconds the millionaire turned to the young man and said, "The reason why you haven't had as much success as you would have liked is because you haven't yet learned to concentrate."

"But I do know how to concentrate," John protested.

"You have no idea what real concentration is."

"All right, tell me, then, what is real concentration?"

"Come closer and look at this bush," the millionaire instructed, turning back toward the bush he'd just smelled.

He pointed out a rose that was much larger, much

more developed, and more beautiful than the others. John obeyed, wondering what the old man was getting at. After looking at the flower for a moment, frowning with the effort, a shy smile on the corners of his lips, John turned to the millionaire and waited for his comments.

"In your opinion," the millionaire asked, "why is this rose larger than the others?"

John shrugged in embarrassment and replied, "Really I . . . I have no idea. I'm not a gardener, and I don't know anything about horticulture."

"Well, it would be a good idea if you did. You'd learn a lot of interesting things about living creatures—and about life in general. All laws can be found in nature, and a person who knows how to read the laws of nature also knows how to read the laws of life. Look at the bush again. Look at this immense rose."

John did as he was told, leaning forward once again to concentrate on the rose as best he could. But once again he could detect nothing out of the ordinary, except that this one rose was larger than all the rest, and wondered if the old man wasn't just having a little fun with him, which would not have surprised him all that much.

"I . . . I really don't know. Maybe it's just a question of luck."

"No," the millionaire said, "what people refer to as

luck does not exist. Luck is only another name for the law of causality, which applies to all things. A positive action or thought, or a correct state of mind, will always inevitably bear fruit, even if it takes time. Because there is a celestial order that is never wrong and overlooks nothing. Simply because there is sometimes quite a gap in time between an action and its result, we tend to forget the cause and concern ourselves only with the effect, which is why we talk about luck. But to get back to our rose here . . . look at it again."

John did as he was told but still saw nothing out of the ordinary. Fine drops of sweat had formed on his forehead. He really felt like an idiot, because he couldn't find any explanation for the flower's exceptional size.

"You don't see anything special?"

"No."

"If you want to succeed in business, or in any other line of work, you're going to have to develop your powers of observation and logic. Many of the millionaires I know would have no trouble finding the answer I want from you, even though they, too, know nothing about horticulture or about roses. People who succeed see details and discover principles that others do not, and that's why ordinary people think they are lucky, while in fact all they are doing is applying laws that are very precise."

The old man pointed to the branch with the spectacular rose and said, "How many flowers are there on this branch?"

The answer was obvious.

"One," John replied.

"And how many on this one?" the millionaire asked, pointing to another branch with a number of medium-sized flowers. John counted them.

"At least a dozen," he said.

"Well, there's your answer. The single rose is larger, not because of luck, but because of the gardener's work, and in fact because of his concentration. Look here," he said. "Come closer."

As John leaned closer to the branch with the dozen flowers, the old "gardener" pointed to a number of tiny buds at its base.

"See here, there are a lot of buds on this branch. I let them grow freely, producing all these flowers." He plucked off one of the buds with his thumb and forefinger. "On this other branch I systematically removed all the buds, just as I did there, allowing only one, the one that looked the most promising, to grow. Thus one flower received all the sap and nutrients contained in the branch and grew to a spectacular size. That is concentration."

John's face lit up.

"The beautiful part about it," the gardener-turned-philosopher went on, anticipating John's train of thought, "is that any one of these buds would have done the same thing if I'd chosen it. That means that any individual can transform his or her life simply by applying the same principle I used on the rosebush. Because there is one important difference between people and other living creatures, and that is that a person can be both the gardener and the rose at the same time!"

CHAPTER 8

*In which
the young man
learns to
concentrate . . .*

THE OLD man walked over to the pond, pulled a piece of bread out of one of the large pockets of his old coat, and started breaking off pieces and throwing them into the water as far away from himself as he could. The ducks all crowded around, fighting for the bread, while the swan, for some reason, ignored the commotion as if he didn't even see the food, almost as if he found it beneath his dignity to eat with the other birds.

"The lives of ordinary people are like the lives of these ducks," the millionaire said. "Every day ordinary people allow themselves to be distracted by friends, relatives, and also by themselves. As soon as they are distracted, they forget. They don't remember that they had a goal in mind. They want one thing one day and

69

something else the next. They run after the little tidbits and games that are tossed their way. Extraordinary people, on the other hand, people who are aware, are like that black swan, which happens to be a symbol of wisdom. They are concentrated, firmly grounded in the center of their being, and nothing can distract them. The willpower of ordinary people is weak because they're nothing more than a series of different little selves, for the most part contradictory. Take yourself, for example. How did you concentrate your efforts at the agency?"

"I must have made hundreds of phone calls trying to drum up some business," John explained.

"To the same person?" the millionaire asked.

"No, of course not! To hundreds of different people. You told me I had to be persevering. So I didn't let myself get discouraged that easily."

The millionaire pursed his lips in disappointment, as if his young disciple hadn't understood a thing he'd taught him.

"When an Eskimo wants to fish through the ice in winter, does he dig a hole by going around and smashing his pick in a hundred different places?"

He didn't have to say any more. John, smiling shamefacedly, had to admit that the lesson was elementary.

"Do you remember the Thomas Edison story?" the millionaire went on. "Did he try to invent ten thousand different things?"

"No," John replied, familiar with the extraordinary perseverance of the celebrated inventor. "It took him ten thousand tries to get the first lightbulb to work."

The two men fell silent for a moment.

"There's one thing that most people forget, or don't even think about," the millionaire continued, "and that's that there's always a reason for failure—just like there's a reason for success. Now, what other mistakes did you make?"

The question took John by surprise.

"I don't know."

"Think about it," the old man insisted. "You know all the answers. You just have to take the trouble to find them."

"I'm really not sure. If I had known at the time, I wouldn't have made them, and I would have been successful."

"Exactly!" the millionaire said, laughing. "I can see that you use your brain at least some of the time. That's a start. But while we're on the subject of thinking, tell me, approximately how much time have you spent just thinking about ways to really succeed since you started your agency?"

"I, uh . . . I must admit . . . I know it's stupid, but I had so much work to do . . ."

"So much work. Like all ordinary people who waste their lives doing useless things instead of stopping and taking the time to think. Pascal said that a man's biggest problem is not being able stay alone in his room. Well, the biggest problem for a businessman—or an artist or a scientist, the profession doesn't matter—is not being able to sit down in the office or the studio or the laboratory with the telephone disconnected, without a secretary or any colleagues around, without any files on the desk, and without letting his own mind distract him, and simply think about how to improve his business or his art; in other words, how to be successful.

"When I started out I understood this secret and spent entire days just thinking, emptying my mind. I shut myself up in my office, unhooked the phone. And I said to myself, 'In a week I'm going to come up with ten lucrative ideas.' The results were phenomenal. In a single week I developed enough ideas, enough projects, to make me more than a million dollars."

"A million dollars?"

"That's right, a million dollars, which I certainly would not have made if I'd spent my time working like everyone else. Obviously I'm not saying you should spend all your time thinking. Some people go too far and never act. They get an idea and then refine it and refine it, until they become paralyzed from too much thinking. There's also a time for action. You have to give it your best shot, and that takes courage and audacity. Once you start something you have to work hard. And I mean intensely, body and soul. Although work isn't the only thing that counts, there's nothing that can take its place. You do have the time if you really try. Real concentration is a sacrifice."

"A sacrifice?" the young man repeated, surprised at this almost religious definition of a more or less common mental activity.

"That's right. Concentrating means sacrificing all other activities. It means directing all your thoughts, all your emotions, all your energy, all the force in your body, nerves, hormones . . . everything toward a single goal. It means making your entire being ardently desire the same thing—and sustaining that desire for days, months, or even years. That's what I call sacrifice.

"As you learn to concentrate, as you devote yourself tirelessly to the same activity, the same profession, you will attain a state in which lucrative ideas, marvelous beneficial ideas, will arise in your mind spontaneously. And once you've attained this state of true concentration, you'll be able to see the crux of every problem almost automatically, like the genius who seems to be able to think without thinking and act without acting. That's why it is said that when you really start making money, a lot of money, you realize that all you have to do is enter a particular state of mind, where whatever you do becomes more like a game than ordinary work. In fact, the real and secret goal of work is to raise your consciousness to a state where everything becomes easy, where riches abound and success is at your fingertips.

"Of course, you will encounter obstacles. Everything in this world, everything in nature, opposes concentration. We live in an age of leisure, of constant distraction. That's why, after a couple of minutes, or ten minutes, or an hour, you forget and start doing something else. Your old self rebels and rears its ugly head up again and again. It's an uphill struggle at first, because you'll be fighting old, ingrained habits that you're probably not even aware of, habits that have been with you for centuries, for millennia! But in time the road will become smoother. Concentration will lead to mental mastery, and mental mastery will allow you to control your destiny. When you're really concentrated you'll develop an immense love for everything you do, you'll become like a child, completely absorbed in what you are occupied with in the present moment, a person for whom the past and future simply do not exist. You'll feel yourself dissolving into this immense love of the present moment, and your triumphs will be all the more remarkable, since whatever we do with love is invariably crowned with success.

"But don't forget that the method I am teaching you must never be used for selfish ends, because whatever you gain at the expense of others will eventually turn against you, strangle you, as surely as if you tried to strangle someone, with a rope that is wrapped around your own neck.

"It is only because the law of causality does not always take effect immediately, often requiring a long passage of time before its results become apparent, that you may think you've gained something when in reality you are only impoverishing yourself. Like a blind man whistling a happy tune as he walks toward a precipice, you may rejoice for a while, thinking you've gotten away with something, only to end up screaming in horror as you fall over the edge."

The old man had run out of bread, and the ducks soon lost interest and swam off. The black swan, which had kept its distance while the ducks were feeding, just as mysteriously approached now that there was no more food.

It stared at the millionaire with an intent yet gentle gaze. The noble bird was almost immobile, and John realized, given the opportunity to observe it from closer up, how beautiful it was. Its eyes, which had an almost human expression, were completely unlike anything he'd ever seen, radiating a kind of great serenity.

The old man took another piece of bread from his pocket and knelt by the edge of the pond. The swan came over and ate from his hand while the millionaire petted it affectionately. The bird was not at all afraid and seemed to enjoy the attention immensely.

Then the swan turned its head and looked at John. He found its gaze extremely disturbing. It was so pure, so full of love, that John suddenly became aware of the smallness of his own life, of his petty desires and hopes. It was as if, in the body of this bird, there resided a soul that was much more evolved than his own.

The old gardener stood up, turned to John, and gave him an encouraging pat on the shoulder, as if he could read his mind.

"You remind me of a lion cub I once read about in an old Indian legend. When it was very young the cub lost his parents and was raised by some goats, so that when he grew up he thought he was a goat, too. He ate like a goat, although he didn't have the right kind of teeth. He tried to bleat like a goat, but his roar sounded all wrong. And when, one day, he met another lion, he didn't recognize his brother and was just as frightened as all the goats were. He had forgotten his true nature, just as most people do. They are lions, acting like goats their whole life long. Those who insist they are lions and not goats are considered fools or prophets by the rest of the herd. Thus I say to you: get rid of the goat so that the lion inside you can awaken!"

Then, as a way of evaluating John's progress, the old man suggested a little test and asked John to concentrate on a rose. John immediately did as he was told, while the millionaire looked on benevolently. After about a minute the millionaire said, "You're doing very well."

The young man, beaming with pride, stopped staring at the rose, faced the millionaire, and said, "Thank you."

"If you'd really been concentrating," the millionaire scolded, "you wouldn't have heard me, and you'd still be staring at the rose. Start again."

Ashamed at having been tricked so easily, John concentrated on the rose once again. "This time," he said to himself, "nothing's going to distract me. Even if he asks me to stop I'll ignore him, I won't move an inch, I won't stop looking at this damn rose. We'll see who's stronger, him or me. He hasn't seen anything yet."

But after some minutes, while John was still completely concentrated, he heard a noise somewhere in front of him, a noise that sounded distinctly like the roaring of a wild animal, a lion or some other kind of wild cat. What's more, the roaring seemed to be coming closer at alarming speed. John abandoned the exercise, looked up, and did indeed see an enormous lion moving toward him in a crouch, as if it were about to pounce on its prey. There was absolutely nothing friendly about the way it was looking at him. John thought he'd lost his mind. What was a lion doing in Southampton, in a rose garden of all places? John turned to the millionaire to see how he was reacting and was astonished to see him standing there, perfectly calmly, as if the savage beast were just a harmless puppy.

"What do we do?" John whispered between clenched teeth.

The millionaire just smiled and said, "If you were really concentrating you wouldn't even have heard the lion coming."

"Right, and I would have been eaten for lunch! Come on!" he said, grabbing the old man's arm, "Let's make a run for it."

"Calm down. There's nothing to be afraid of."

The lion, now only a few feet away, stopped roaring and rubbed up against the old man's leg. The millionaire stroked the animal's fur, plunging his fingers into its thick mane while the lion purred with pleasure.

"Good boy, Horace, you're a good boy."

John looked on in amazement.

"You see, John," the millionaire said, "you got all worked up over nothing. When your mind becomes stronger, better trained, when you've learned to see things clearly, you'll understand that we *always* worry over nothing, and that everything that happens has a reason. Things always happen for the best. And at the same time, in a way, nothing is really of any importance. Things are only as important as we make them. So the next time you're beset with a situation that appears very serious, or even insurmountable, remember what I just told you and think about what just happened here. One day you'll realize that these problems are just misunderstandings, traps we fall into because we haven't mastered our own mind. Even death, the supreme problem, which so many people are terrified of, is a completely harmless, insignificant phenomenon. The world is simply a reflection of your mind. If your mind remains perfectly calm, even under the most critical circumstances, even when faced with death, all your anxiety will disappear and all your problems will dissolve back into the void whence they arose. Think about it. Think hard. When you've understood this principle, you'll be free. And you'll enjoy a much greater kind of freedom than a bank account with millions of dollars in it can give you."

After a few moments the old man slapped the lion

on the haunch and it trotted back the way it had come, this time without roaring, to John's immense relief. As he watched it move away he wondered what other surprises the eccentric millionaire had in store for him.

CHAPTER 9

In which
the young man
discovers the power
of faith . . .

WHEN THE lion had disappeared down the pathway, the old man pointed to the curious metal sphere in the middle of the pond and said, "When your willpower has grown strong through the practice of concentration, you'll be able to accomplish great things. In fact, you'll be able to set this sphere spinning."

John looked skeptical. It sounded like some kind of magic trick. He knew the millionaire was wise, that he possessed great mental powers, but to be able to set a metal sphere turning just by concentrating on it . . .

"Try it."

The young man pursed his lips. It really was a strange request, another trap perhaps. The old man had clearly demonstrated, since their very first encounter, that he had a number of tricks up his sleeve.

John cast a questioning glance at the millionaire, as if to make certain that he was serious about this new and strange exercise. The millionaire nodded with a smile. John did as he was told—he tried to concentrate on the sphere and make it spin, but of course he failed. He turned back to the millionaire, who said, "What makes thinking powerful is the fusion of the large with the small self. To make this happen, one of the best, fastest, and simplest methods is to repeat one of the great magic formulas, such as *'Day by day, in every way, I am getting better and better.'* Or this one, which I've been using for years: *'Day by day, in all ways, I am more powerful, confident, healthy, and happy.'* These formulations are the secret keys to unlocking your inner power, to awakening your inner wisdom, which I mentioned earlier. Your mind is like Aladdin's lamp. To awaken your own slumbering genie just repeat these great formulations and the miracle will take place. Little by little, you will start becoming who you really are, as you realize that your lamp is your mind and you are your own genie. You are both master and servant, only you don't know it. As you discover your inner wisdom you will find yourself, although you were never really lost. You were like a woman who finds around her own neck a necklace she's looked for everywhere. Can she say the necklace was lost? Most people, in the name of realism, let real life pass them by. They forget about their great dreams and tell themselves, 'You have to be realistic,' when, in fact, real life is nothing but magic, pure magic, because the human mind can accomplish anything, and I mean anything in the literal sense of the word. All your inner wisdom needs is a word from you to prove it."

The millionaire fell silent and turned toward the sphere. His expression grew serious. His eyes, which always shined, seemed to light up with even more fiery intensity. And to John's great astonishment, after just a few seconds the sphere began turning.

John thought he was dreaming. Finally here was proof, in the form of a concrete demonstration, that the mind possessed infinite power. Shivers ran up and down his spine, and he was overcome with a kind of religious awe, as invariably happens to people who experience phenomena that are beyond the scope of common understanding.

And yet a seed of doubt sprang up in his mind. What if the old man, a veritable master of the art of illusion, had rigged up some kind of remote control device, stepping on a certain stone, for example . . . Or what if it was just the wind?

John looked around the sphere, but the water in the pond was perfectly still, disturbed only by the ducks' slow paddling. As for wind, well, the rosebushes were immobile.

The sphere began spinning more and more rapidly, and soon the eight bands it was made of fused into one solid mass. As it spun even more quickly it suddenly appeared to be standing still. There was not a hint of a breeze.

Then he heard a mysterious and beautiful sound, like the deep chorus of a celestial choir—or, more precisely, the slow repetition of the mantra "Om," reputed to be the primordial sound. John listened attentively, feeling more and more uneasy. He couldn't say why, but he felt the music communing directly with his soul, a feeling he had already experienced in the past when, for example, he had listened to some particularly moving piece of music, or when he'd witnessed a sublime sunset or a night sky studded with millions of stars. He felt as if he were overlooking something extremely important.

He wondered how many precious moments he'd overlooked, if it wasn't a part of his character to always neglect the essential things in life, the really important things, postponing them for later, as so often happens with the people you love—there never seems to be enough time to express the great passions we feel, so we keep putting things off. And then one day it's too late, they're gone, lost, it's our own fault, and we know we'll never see them again. John's eyes filled with tears.

As if to add to the magic of the scene, a flock of beautiful birds, arriving from who knows where, swooped down and started circling the sphere. Perhaps they, like John, were entranced by the heavenly music.

The ducks also seemed attracted by the strange sound and formed a circle in the water around the sphere, tilting their heads in a curious manner, as if perplexed or in some kind of ecstatic trance.

After about a minute the intensity of the music diminished and the sphere started slowing down until it stopped completely. The flock of birds, numbering close to a hundred, immediately flew off, flying in a curious single-file formation, like the birds in the paintings of Hieronymus Bosch.

"One day," the millionaire said, rousing John from his reverie, "you, too, will be able to set the sphere spinning and produce this celestial music. When you do, you will have considerable power, but remember that your power should always be used for what is right and good, both for you and for others. Never use your power for selfish or harmful purposes. If you do, the law of causality will turn against you. Always abide by the great golden rule: do unto others as you would have them do unto you. And if you can, take the law one step further, pushing it to the limit: do nothing for yourself and everything for others. This supreme devotion, which I say is the aim of all existence, will endow you with great power. You will appear to be the smallest, most modest of men, while in reality you will be among the greatest. In the future, whenever you feel unhappy, know that it is because you have forgotten this great principle and have reverted to your old selfish ways. Get rid of your old self, as you would of a useless old winter coat in springtime, and you'll soon be roaming the white sandy beaches of the Isle of Happiness."

The millionaire paused for a moment and then said, "Try to make the sphere spin one more time. I'll just take a walk around while you do."

Without knowing why, John felt slightly intoxicated, as if the rose garden had the same effect as the famous island of the lotus eaters in Homer's *Odyssey*. He sat down on one of the stone benches bordering the pond and began concentrating on the sphere as the old man headed slowly down the pathway.

John could still hardly believe that the old man had been able to spin the sphere simply by using his willpower. And yet a distant and mysterious voice, somewhere in the depths of his being, a voice from his most ancient past, seemed to murmur like a fragrant breeze that perhaps it wasn't all that impossible, that perhaps this power was not beyond his capabilities after all.

He straightened his back, having read a couple of es-
oteric books that claimed that a person's energy circulated better when the spine was straight, and stared at
the sphere with all the intensity he could muster. He
didn't know quite how to proceed, so he began sending
mental commands to it, as if it were a living being, a re-
bellious pet he was trying to train, repeating the
thought over and over again in his mind: "Now, sphere,
you will start turning!"

But the sphere seemed oblivious to his orders and remained perfectly still. John kept it up for a few long
minutes, after which he began to feel discouraged. He
yawned and massaged his forehead, as if he felt a
headache coming on. But then he thought that his real
problem had always been a lack of perseverance, that
the secret of genius resides in being infinitely patient,
that he always tended to give up too soon, perhaps,
without even knowing it, just when he was about to
succeed. So he concentrated once more, and it was
then, to his great astonishment, that the sphere actually started spinning, slowly at first, and then faster and
faster until the celestial music could be heard once
again.

He felt a mixture of pride and joy at his unexpected
success. If he could make material objects move simply
by using the power of his mind, what could he not ac-

complish in the future? Nothing was beyond his capabilities. He would enjoy one success after another.

He felt ecstatically happy, as if he'd suddenly discovered that he possessed some superhuman power. He sprang to his feet, climbed onto the stone bench, and, raising his arms to the heavens, began a little dance of joy. But as he twirled around he saw the millionaire standing there watching him, blue eyes glittering with a metallic, mocking sheen. John's bubble of enthusiasm deflated like a popped balloon and he lowered his arms, realizing that it had been the old man, and not he, who had set the sphere spinning.

"Practice makes perfect!" the millionaire remarked.

His cheeks purple with embarrassment, John climbed down off the bench and stammered, "I . . . I thought you were taking a walk—"

"If you really believe," the old gardener interrupted him, "you will succeed. Faith can move mountains. Unfortunately, most people think that seeing is believing. To really succeed you need real faith, faith that allows you to see what you want to attain even before attaining it, like a farmer who holds a few seeds in his hands and sees the golden stalks of wheat that will fill his fields by the end of summer. Because real faith isn't what most people think it is. Real faith is simply an inner vision of great spiritual laws. Spiritual people may appear to believe in something, but in reality all they are doing is seeing what is invisible to ordinary people, just as easily as you see the rosebushes around us and, with total confidence, can assure a blind person that they exist. All millionaires have this kind of faith at the start of their careers, which is why they are so often accused of being fools or dreamers."

They stood and watched the sphere in the middle of the pond slowing down. When it stopped completely the old man continued.

"But faith isn't everything. You also need audacity, you need to dare to achieve the things you really want and not let fear bury your talents, as so many people do. Take you, for example. Why are you afraid to do what you really want to do? But never mind that now," he said before John could reply. "Let me show you around the house."

John, still in a state of mild shock after the strange phenomenon he had just witnessed, followed the millionaire out of the garden. As they passed the withered rosebush at the garden's entrance the millionaire paused a moment and, in a sadly enigmatic voice, uttered, "You see, John, every time I pass this rosebush I think of you. . . ."

CHAPTER 10

In which
the young man
is nostalgic . . .

As EVENING fell, Henry, the butler, showed John to his room, leading him up a sumptuous stairway, its walls literally lined with paintings. All the paintings except one, the first one, depicted famous personalities. The sole exception was apparently a portrait of an Oriental sage named Nityananda, a thin young man, almost emaciated, wrapped in a white shawl, whose gaze had a celestial softness to it. A caption under the painting read, "Find God in your heart."

His immediate neighbor, Jesus, clad in a white tunic, pointed at heaven, saying, "Awaken and pray." Next to him was the great philosopher Plato, climbing the steps of a Greek temple and declaring, "No serious man speaks seriously about serious matters." The resemblance between Plato and his neighbor, Leonardo da Vinci, struck John for the first time. The universal Renaissance genius claimed, "To be your own master, you must be alone."

There was a reproduction of the Mona Lisa, and next to it a portrait of the inventor of the automobile, Henry Ford, addressing members of his board of directors, gazing at them with his penetrating eyes and declaring, "Everything I did, I did only to demonstrate the power of faith. Anything we believe we can accomplish can be accomplished."

There was also a magnificent portrait of the old millionaire himself, standing in the middle of his rose garden. Not surprisingly, his words of wisdom concerned his favorite flowers: "Everything resides in the heart of the rose."

John was surprised to see that the last picture in this illustrious collection depicted none other than Stephen Spielberg's famous character E.T., pointing his long, luminous finger at the sky, staring at the heavens with large nostalgic eyes, saying, "E.T. call 'om,' . . ." with the word *home* having been intentionally replaced by the single-syllable mantra "om."

Henry left John at the door of his room, an immense suite twice as large as his whole apartment. Sliding doors opened onto a balcony, and a circular bed occupied the center of the room, the floor of which was covered by a carpet so thick that John thought if he lost a shoe he'd probably have trouble finding it again! Two lion's heads appeared to be standing guard over the large black fireplace, where a fire had already been lit.

John immediately went out onto the balcony, which had a view of the millionaire's magnificent rose garden running down to the seashore. The water was calm, reflecting the silvery light of the full moon. Inspired by the gentle sea breeze, John began thinking about the incredible journey he'd just had, the strange philosophy lesson in front of the withered rosebush, discovering the spinning sphere and the millionaire's lion, Horace . . .

His thoughts turned to Rachel, and worries similar to those he'd felt when she'd left began haunting him. What was she doing at that moment? What was the real reason for her trip to Boston? Did she really need time to think, as she'd said? Or was she trying to let him down easy, prepare him for a permanent separation she'd been planning for a long time?

He knew very well that things weren't the same as when they'd met. He thought about their first night together. To celebrate the only lucrative contract he'd managed to land, John had invited Rachel, who was still only his assistant at the time, to the Plaza Hotel.

The prestigious Fifth Avenue hotel was having a

"retro night" that evening. Nostalgic couples showed up in great numbers to listen to 1940s' music, played by a very competent band with a small brass section.

Rachel adored dancing. Her feet seemed to have wings, and her whole body seemed to come alive whenever she heard the first few bars of a tune she liked. She had a particular affinity for the music of that era, which made for a happy coincidence.

When the band started playing the first chords of Nat King Cole's "Unforgettable," Rachel felt overcome with nostalgia, as the song brought back a host of memories. It had been her parents' favorite. They'd always been very close. Rachel knew the words by heart.

"Shall we dance?" John asked.

He had never excelled as a dancer, but the champagne helped—he hadn't skimped on the wining and dining, intending to impress Rachel and at the same time thank her for the important role she'd played in landing the contract—and he managed to forget his complex about being clumsy, which was aggravated whenever he danced with a tall woman, especially one as stunning as Rachel. They headed for the dance floor.

There certainly seemed to be a special chemistry at work between them, a kind of profound harmony despite the difference in their height, which was all the more apparent because of Rachel's high heels. They made a beautiful couple. In any case, they did not go unnoticed on the dance floor, since, it must be said, they were by far the youngest couple there, most of the others having reached retirement age.

"They're all so charming, aren't they?" Rachel, who had always had a weakness for older couples, said.

"Yes."

"Look at those two," she said, directing John's attention to a couple who were at least in their seventies, possibly in their eighties, but who still moved very elegantly together, dancing cheek to cheek like a pair of lovebirds. "They look like they just got engaged."

"You're right, they're adorable," John said, also feeling nostalgic as he thought about his own parents.

Because of his lack of dancing experience he had to make an effort not to appear too clumsy. At the same time he found Rachel's perfume, and the simple fact of holding her in his arms, of feeling her body pressing against his for the first time, extremely troubling.

He had often thought about asking her out to a movie (her favorite pastime) or for a drink after work. In fact, he had fallen madly in love with her the day he hired her but had always held back, thinking it would be better not to become too intimate with his assistant. After all, it would be a mistake to get involved with an employee, wouldn't it? And what about her feelings toward him? Could they continue working together if she didn't feel the same way? Wouldn't a declaration of love create a highly embarrassing situation for them both? Was it worth the risk of losing a precious helper like her?

And yet on a number of occasions he had caught Rachel looking at him in a certain way, a way that seemed to betray a certain feeling, or at least some interest on her part. But how could he know for sure? In the end his indecision had not prevented him from making a romantic, if not completely illogical gesture: he went out and bought an engagement ring at Tiffany's, the prestigious Fifth Avenue jeweler's, persuaded that doing so would bring him luck.

Rachel pressed up against him, as if she felt his distress, or as if she herself was troubled. He very gently held her at arm's length, and for a few long moments they looked into each other's eyes. John felt there was no turning back, that Rachel's gaze held a promise, an avowal of her love for him.

But by the time the end of the evening rolled around he had neither kissed her nor declared his love for her. She lived in Brooklyn, as he did, a coincidence John interpreted as another stroke of destiny. As they left the hotel they heard thunder growling in the sky overhead, but John decided not to put the top up on his convertible, thinking he'd have time to drive Rachel home before the storm broke.

He was wrong. They had hardly set out when the storm—or destiny—struck.

John hurriedly pulled over and tried to get the top up, but it got stuck. By the time he was able to fix the mechanism both he and Rachel were soaked to the skin. Rachel didn't seem to mind. In fact, she started laughing, her hair pasted down on her forehead, as if she found the whole incident highly amusing. Thunderclaps kept rumbling overhead every few seconds, and John, out of a sense of safety, said, "This could be dangerous. Let's go to my place, it's just a couple of blocks from here. When the storm's over I'll drive you home."

She made no objection. He drove home, and they hurried up to his apartment, where they dried themselves off as best they could. John noticed that Rachel's mascara had started running and burst out laughing.

"What's so funny?" she asked.

"Oh, nothing, it's just your eyes—your cheeks, actually . . ."

She looked around for a mirror and found one hanging in the living room. Upon seeing her reflection she thought she looked a sorry state.

"Wait," John said, walking over with a handkerchief.

He began wiping her eyes, once again troubled by the odor of her perfume, which the rain had intensified. After that everything happened very quickly.

Rachel kicked off her high heels, which she'd regretted wearing all evening. Now that she was a couple of inches shorter, and certain that the difference would inspire John with confidence, she took his hand as if to say that she couldn't care less about her mascara and that the time had come to get down to more serious matters. She stared intensely into his eyes.

John understood that if he didn't kiss her then and there, he might be passing up the perfect opportunity to break the ice with her. The magic of the evening they'd just spent together would never repeat itself. Rachel might think he didn't feel anything for her and start looking around for another man. He stopped thinking, refusing to allow his doubts to impede him any further.

Outside, a tremendous clap of thunder resounded and the power suddenly cut out, plunging the apartment into darkness. Rachel cried out in fear. John pressed her to him and then, finally, dared to kiss her for the first time. They were soon embracing on the floor, having gotten rid of their soaking clothes, and their union was so profound that both found themselves crying tears of joy, as if they'd found each other again after too long an absence.

After their lovemaking they lay together for a long time, united by a great, almost religious emotion. Tenderly they caressed each other's faces, skin, and hair without saying anything. But their ecstasy was rudely interrupted as the electricity suddenly came back on and light flooded the apartment.

They both burst out laughing, and their laughter grew until they were rolling around like a couple of children. When the moment finally subsided, John sprang to his feet, full of renewed energy.

"I'm hungry," he declared.

For the first time in a long time he looked happy. He disappeared into the kitchen, still completely naked, as Rachel admired the lines of his body.

She also felt recharged from their lovemaking. She got up and started looking around.

Her explorations led her to a wooden chest of drawers standing near the entrance. There were a number of objects on it: John's keys, a pile of unopened mail, a couple of office files, and some pretty knickknacks. Among these she noticed a little Tiffany box. She felt a kind of shock. It was as if she knew right away what the box contained. She hurriedly opened it to see if her intuition was correct, and it was.

The engagement ring literally took her breath away. "Tiffany's!" she thought, overcome with emotion. "He's crazy. He must have paid a fortune for it! Does that mean he loves me completely?"

John, returning from the kitchen, where he'd found nothing to eat, surprised her with the box in her hand. Embarrassed, he coughed discreetly so Rachel would know he was there.

Rachel quickly shut the box and took a few steps away, stopping in front of a reproduction that she pretended to be interested in. Still naked, John walked up and took her in his arms. He kissed her cheek and said, "There's absolutely nothing in this damn apartment to eat. I can order something. What would you like?"

"What I'd really like to eat?" she said suggestively, lowering her eyes and looking at John.

"Yes, what you'd *really* want to eat."

She paused as if to heighten the effect of her little game, pouting mischievously, and finally replied, "A big pastrami sandwich!"

The vision of this scene haunted John's mind for a moment. How simple things were back then, actually such a short time ago! What had happened? Why had he still not asked Rachel to marry him? Why had he still not offered her the ring he'd paid so dearly for, which she, out of a sense of tact, had never mentioned?

He left the balcony and returned to his room. Seeing a phone, he decided to give Rachel a call. Who knows, maybe she'd come back sooner than planned, cutting short her stay in Boston. He let the phone ring a few times, but then her answering machine cut in. He listened to the message religiously. How beautiful her voice was, so warm and bright. He hung up without leaving a message.

CHAPTER 11

In which
the young man
learns the secret
meaning of life . . .

THE NEXT day John awoke at seven, his room flooded with sunlight, the air fragrant with the smell of a bouquet of roses that he hadn't noticed the night before, unless someone had brought it without his knowing during the night or in the early hours of the morning. He took a quick shower, got dressed, and went down to the dining room, where a tablecloth had already been laid. Plates, bowls, and utensils all shone with the glint of gold, accentuating the immaculate whiteness of the tablecloth.

John didn't dare sit down right away. He noticed a little bell on the table, rang it, and waited. But no one appeared, which he found strange, since the night before a number of servants had been busy around the house. He rang the bell again, to no avail, and then, since he was dying for some food, and since there was a box of cereal on the table, he decided to start on his own.

To his surprise, as soon as he sat down some very beautiful classical music, Bach's Overture in C Major, started playing, resounding off the dining room's gold-paneled walls. He jumped out of the chair in surprise, and the music stopped.

He examined the chair, actually a small armchair, and he pressed down on the seat cushion. The music began again. John smiled, admiring the millionaire's blatant love of luxury.

He sat down again, charmed by the strains of the Bach concerto, and served himself a generous portion of cereal drowned in milk. But as soon as he picked up the beautiful golden spoon he heard a curious lapping sound.

Intrigued, he examined the spoon, wondering if it, too, was not equipped with a secret mechanism, like the chair. But all he saw was the distorted reflection of his nasal appendage. He placed the spoon back on the table and was surprised when the lapping sound ceased. But then it started up again and, leaning over to his left, John finally discovered where it was coming from.

Under the table he saw a beautiful little lion cub lapping milk from a large golden bowl. The little beast, its whiskers all white, wearing a red knit jacket, its tail twitching, frolicked around joyously, looking like the happiest little animal in the whole world.

John was charmed by the image for a moment, and then, hoping the cub's father wouldn't show up, hurriedly gulped down his cereal and took his leave of the little carnivore, heading out to the garden, where he hoped to find the old millionaire.

"Why aren't you doing what you really want to do? What's holding you back?" The old man, who was, in fact, in the rose garden, where he spent almost all his mornings, resumed the grilling he'd begun the day before, not bothering with preliminaries.

The question was asked without animosity, without any trace of irony, but with the authority that, in the old man, was simply a mask of affection. The unexpectedly serious query buzzed through John's mind. Why wasn't he doing what he really wanted to do? Why had he buried his talents instead of using them to prosper?

"Are you afraid of something?"

"No. Well . . . yes, maybe a little . . . because my dream, what I really want to do, is to . . ." He hesitated, but finally blurted it out. "What I really want to do is write a script, a script that would make a great movie. But I don't know if I can make any money doing that. It

isn't easy. . . . I don't know anyone in the business, and
I've never written a script before. . . ."

"Do you think it would be any harder than going to
the moon?"

"No, I . . ."

"You can make money doing anything. There are
thousands of examples that prove this law. You just
have to dare to be yourself and listen to your inner
voice. Because every person is on this earth for a precise
reason. But when I say 'precise,' I don't mean that
everyone is aware of what the reason is. In fact, just
how conscious a person is of that reason is directly re-
lated to how evolved they are, how old their soul is.
The older an incarnated soul is, the more it preserves a
precise memory of what it is supposed to be doing on
Earth. That's one of the reasons so many prodigies and
geniuses, whose souls are well advanced on the path,
are often extremely precocious and have, from the age
of four or five onward, a very precise idea of what they
want to do in life. For most people, the plan generally
becomes apparent much later on. However, it is reassur-
ing to know that since life plans are determined by our
souls and by our guides before we are incarnated, we almost invariably find ourselves living under conditions
and in situations that are conducive to the realization
of our ambitions. Even the obstacles we encounter on

the way, persons who apparently complicate our lives and oppose our plans, are in fact there to help us. They help build character, affirm our faith, and test our perseverance. Because life is nothing more than an immense temple, a kind of initiation ritual in which all souls are each other's masters.

"Less developed souls, still encumbered by the obscurities of the exterior world, must delve into themselves and ask for help, sincerely, because as it is said, 'Ask and ye shall receive, knock and ye shall be admitted.' It often happens that a soul, in a moment of distress, is suddenly struck by its own inner light, suddenly understanding the profound perfection of its situation, that help is already at hand, subtle and mysterious . . . that help has always been there, only we were not aware of it. Because our guides generally work in ways that we do not fathom. What seems to us a terrible ordeal is often the quickest way—sometimes the only way in the time allotted to us—to help us evolve, to refine our character until it once again becomes what it has always been, an immortal diamond shining like the light of a thousand suns. Take yourself, for example. Who do you think you are? Where would you place yourself on the scale of souls?"

"I know what I want, but I . . ."

"Knowing intuitively what you want, having that inner certitude, is already an important step. But now, if you want to accomplish your destiny, you have to be daring. You have to have the audacity to become who you are. Because nobody can do that for you. And if you don't do it, no matter how many material possessions you accumulate, no matter how outwardly successful you are, you'll always be bothered by a feeling of having failed. It will eat away at you your whole life long, and just as surely as cancer destroys your body, it will destroy whatever joy you have."

John listened attentively. No one had ever spoken to him like this before. The millionaire's words seemed to be coming from somewhere very far away, as far as his own soul. How was it that the old man seemed to see through him with such disturbing lucidity?

The millionaire continued.

"Your life plan is not simply to write scripts, which would be a vain undertaking. What you write has to reveal what is great about humanity. You have to show how people can attain their own greatness, how they can regain their lost nobility, how, having turned into sheep, they can become lions once again.

"Show that God resides in each and every one of us, and that every time we forget, every time we see our lives and the lives of others in a different light, we become the artisans of our own unhappiness.

"Show that by constantly maintaining an ideal of perfection, of greatness, of light and love, we can accomplish our destiny, surrounding ourselves with the kind of energy that will keep us young, beautiful, luminous, and open the marvelous doorway to all achievement.

"Show people that they can live perfect lives, lives of abundance where everything occurs in its right time and place, where the cup of eternal wine is always full and cannot be emptied or even diminished by even the most greedy of lips.

"On many occasions you will be tempted to stray from your path, because it's sometimes very difficult to stick to your life plan. But if you do, you will not be happy. So return, with courage. And every time you are unhappy, tell yourself that it is probably a sign you have deviated from your plan.

"Look inward, ask your inner wisdom, and your guides, for advice, and then wait for an answer. In the meantime, do something positive for another person, help someone. In this way you will accumulate merit and provide for your own future happiness, just as surely as a farmer stores up his grain in summer for the long winter months ahead. And remember that the greatest service, the ultimate service, is to teach others to discover the truth, which is the only thing that can set them free and make them happy."

Henry, the butler, walked up to them and asked if they wished to have lunch.

"We'll be drinking a glass of farewell wine together, my dear Henry," the millionaire said.

"Very good, sir," Henry replied, and took his leave.

With these words John realized, not without some sadness, that his marvelous visit with the millionaire was coming to an end. However, he had no reason to complain, as he felt he'd already taken advantage of his host's generosity.

The millionaire then asked John to show him his palm. Intrigued, but not daring to question him, John obeyed, holding out his right hand.

"No, your left hand," the old man said. He studied John's palm attentively before letting go of it. Then, after a moment of silence, as if he were trying to interpret the signs he'd just read in the young man's hand, he said, "It will take time, a lot of time, before you realize your ambitions."

"Why?" John asked with a note of discouragement.

"Because your nature still lacks discipline."

"Isn't there a way to speed things up?" the young man said, trying to be practical.

"Yes, but there is a price to pay as well."

"I'm ready to pay anything."

The millionaire emitted a strange laugh.

"You talk without thinking. If you knew what the price was, you wouldn't be so quick to decide."

"Tell me, then."

"I cannot reveal it to you. You'll discover what the price is when the time comes. That is a law I cannot circumvent. But I can do something if you *really* want to speed things up. . . ."

After a moment's hesitation John, in a feverish voice, unable to measure the impact of the statement he was about to make, said, "I really do."

The millionaire considered the request for a moment, as if to sound out the sincerity of John's desire. Then, apparently satisfied, he rang for the servant and said simply, "I'll see what I can do."

He walked a few steps to a stone table that John had not noticed before. Shortly after the two men took their places, Henry returned with a carafe of wine, sculpted in gold and encrusted with precious stones, and two golden wineglasses that looked like ancient chalices. He set the glasses on the table and filled them with wine.

"Let's drink now," the millionaire said.

The two men emptied their glasses. Then the millionaire stood up, and John understood that the time for his departure had come.

"When will we see each other again?"

"At the right time," the millionaire said with a smile. "Henry, you may go."

A few minutes later John, ready to leave, holding the wooden box containing the old radio that the millionaire had given him the night before, stood on the mansion's front steps with his mentor. Edgar pulled up in the limousine, opened the passenger door, and waited. Before climbing in, John shook the old man's hand and thanked him for all he'd done for him. The old man, who seemed never to do anything like everybody else, clasped John's hand between both of his own and held it for a very long time. He stared into John's eyes with his profoundly mysterious, extraordinarily luminous gaze and, just before letting go of his hand, in a serious voice, as if pronouncing a final farewell, said, "You will succeed. Never give up. Never. Never."

CHAPTER 12

In which the young man's destiny is accomplished...

JOHN CLIMBED into the backseat of the limo. As it pulled away he stared back at the old millionaire, who was standing on the steps of his mansion, waving and smiling with nostalgia, as if he were watching his own son depart. When the old man was lost from view, John admired the beauty of his host's property one last time.

As they headed for the front gates he saw Horace walking slowly in a field with the little lion cub gamboling along behind him. He also saw a lioness, the cub's mother, he supposed, completing what appeared to be a perfect family.

He lowered the window. With his hair blowing in the wind and the old wooden box he had been given on his knees, he felt uplifted by his stay at the millionaire's house and by the old man's assurance that he would succeed and become a screenwriter.

And he recalled what the millionaire had told him about the box and the radio it contained: "Everything the human mind conceives of and believes in can be accomplished." "So," John said to himself, "if I really believe I can become a screenwriter and sell my scripts, I can do it, and nothing can stop me."

Before long, the chauffeur dropped him off at his apartment. Compared to the mansion he'd just visited, his own domicile looked very shabby. John couldn't help thinking that if what the millionaire had predicted came true, he, too, might one day live in a luxurious mansion.

He put the wooden box on the set of drawers in the entrance, noticing a carton of Marlboros, his favorite brand of cigarettes, and suddenly remembering that he hadn't had a smoke for hours, hadn't even thought about smoking, in fact. "Amazing," he thought.

He called Rachel, but she hadn't returned. It wasn't until the following day, as he entered his office, that he found her already at work. He was overjoyed to see her, but he was still a little worried about what she might have decided on her journey. Did she want them to separate? Or was she ready to give it a second chance, even though they'd been struggling for some time now?

She rose to greet him, and he threw his arms around her neck, holding her close, closer than he'd ever held her before, almost to the point of suffocating her. He had a terrible desire to tell her how much he loved her, that he'd never loved another woman as much, but his shyness held him back, a kind of superstitious fear that he'd ruin everything by declaring his passion.

"I missed you so much," he said.

"Me, too."

"It feels like centuries since you left."

"You mean I look older?" she teased, running a hand over her cheek as if time had tarnished her satin skin.

"No," he said, "and I'll prove it to you."

He hurried over to the door and hung a BACK IN FIVE MINUTES sign, which he sometimes used when he had to step out, on the handle.

"Five centuries or five minutes?" Rachel teased again, as John pushed her down on her desk, which she hadn't even had time to clear. The telephone rang just as they melted into each other, swept away by the throes of their passion.

"Blake Agency," Rachel answered, doing her best to control her heaving breath. "Yes. No, I just climbed a flight of stairs. Thanks, no problem, my heart's still in pretty good shape. No, he's busy with a client right now. But I don't think there'll be a problem. If you'd care to hold on a minute, I'll check his schedule."

She put a hand over the receiver and pretended to consult an imaginary agenda, and after an appropriate pause she said, "No, he's free. No problem. Oh, yes, he's very busy these days. But I'm sure he'll come up with something just as brilliant as last time. I'll tell him as soon as he comes back. . . . I mean, as soon as he's out of his meeting."

She hung up and burst out laughing, as did John; then she sighed and, running a hand through his hair, said, "This is much better than a cup of coffee in the morning to wake me up!"

"It sure is."

"That was Mr. Rogers. Remember him?"

"Yeah, our only paying client."

"He wants you to stop by his office this afternoon. It sounds important."

"All right! I knew things would pick up."

Rachel gave John a puzzled look.

"I saw the old millionaire while you were away. He told me that I would succeed, that I could make that dream I told you about come true."

"Writing a screenplay?"

"Yeah."

"I knew that. I told you, but you didn't believe me."

"That's true . . . I . . . but now I know it's possible. I even know what I want to write about. I'll just tell people the story of how I met the old millionaire. He's an extraordinary guy, a real magician. What I plan to do is divide my time in half. I'll spend a couple of days a week on my writing and the rest of the time I'll devote to the agency."

"Sounds like a great idea."

Rachel looked at John lovingly, feeling so glad to see him happy again, the first time since his father had died. Taking that little trip had turned out to be a good idea after all. The separation had seemed to reignite John's waning passion. She was sure it wouldn't be long now before he popped the big question and offered her the magnificent engagement ring she'd seen in his apartment on their first night together.

As she buttoned up her jacket Rachel suddenly grew very pale and fell into the nearest chair.

"Are you all right?" John asked.

"It's a good thing we had only five minutes. You almost killed me."

"No, seriously, are you okay?"

"It's nothing," she said with some embarrassment. "I didn't have breakfast this morning, I must need some sugar or something. I think I'm hypoglycemic. That's what my friend in Boston told me. . . ."

"Don't move. I'll get you some juice," John said as he darted out the door.

After a quick stop at the corner store, John hurried

back to the agency with some juice and a few sweet buns and forced Rachel to eat. She was pleased with the attention he was giving her, with the way he seemed to genuinely care for her, and after swallowing a few mouthfuls she felt much better and smiled.

"You've got to take better care of yourself."

"I know," Rachel said.

There was a short silence, which John interrupted by saying, "I think we should have a talk."

"Sure," said Rachel, "I . . ."

"Maybe tomorrow night we could . . . you could come over for dinner if you like . . ."

"All right" was all Rachel said, although the two simple words were charged with emotion.

That afternoon, as John was running to catch a taxi to take him to his meeting with Mr. Rogers, the client who had called that morning, he fell flat on his face.

He thought he must have tripped over something or left one of his shoelaces untied, but upon further inspection he realized that that was not the case. He'd just fallen down, for no apparent reason. "Damn," he thought. "What's going on? Am I forgetting how to walk?" He got up and stood there on the sidewalk like a child about to take its first hesitant steps, wondering if he was going to fall again if he tried to move. He took a tentative step, but his legs felt shaky, as if they were made of rubber, and would not respond to his commands.

He managed to limp over to a bench and sat down to rest, by now very worried. What was wrong with him? He'd never had any problems with his legs before, and after all he was hardly an old man. He felt extremely anxious, but after a few minutes his strength seemed to return and he got up and shook his legs, feeling somewhat reassured. It must have been a false alarm, maybe the result of accumulated fatigue. He found he could walk completely normally once again.

He hailed another taxi and was soon in his client's office. An hour later, as he left the client's building, he felt the same weakness in his legs coming on and crumpled to the ground. This time he wasn't even running, so he couldn't have tripped or slipped, and both his shoelaces were tied. Something was definitely wrong.

A few pedestrians formed a circle around him. One man, displaying the skepticism so characteristic of New Yorkers—after all, John could have been just another pickpocket looking for a mark—leaned over cautiously and said, "Are you all right?"

"It's probably a heart attack," declared an elderly woman. "Someone should call an ambulance."

"No, no," John said. "I'm okay. . . ."

But then he thought that maybe she was right, that

even though he'd felt no pains in his chest—or any other symptoms, for that matter—he might have had a mild heart attack.

He placed a hand over his heart. The man leaning over him concluded that the old woman's diagnosis was correct and reached down to loosen John's tie. John, who was wearing his father's tie, reacted somewhat aggressively and pushed the man's hands away, absurdly fearing that he intended to steal it for some reason.

"Don't touch me!" John cried. "I said I'm okay. I'm fine, really."

The man, who hadn't been sure about helping John in the first place, stood up and walked away without another word, muttering under his breath that people in New York were all idiots and that he really should act on his plan to move out of this infernal city, as far away as possible from the twelve million nut cases who inhabited it.

John tried to get to his feet, but only managed to make it to his knees before falling again. He was as puzzled as he was distressed. What the hell was going on? An ambulance arrived, and he kept telling the medics that he was fine, that everything was under control. However, since he was incapable of taking a step without falling, they convinced him to let them take him to the hospital for a checkup.

He was kept overnight. He called Rachel from his

hospital bed to tell her that he probably wouldn't be at the agency next morning because he had to go back and see Mr. Rogers, but that he was still on for dinner tomorrow evening. He didn't mention anything about falling, not wanting her to worry for nothing.

Late the next afternoon, after spending the day undergoing a series of tests, he was visited by a certain Dr. Grant.

"You're suffering from a spinal aneurism," Dr. Grant said.

"Spinal aneurism? What does that mean?"

"It would take too long to explain in detail. Let's just say that a few blood vessels in your spine burst—"

"Is it serious?"

"Yes, it is."

"When will I be able to walk again?"

"I can't tell you that. There is a risk you may never walk normally again. In the meantime we'll set you up with a wheelchair and a pair of crutches."

"A wheelchair? Does that mean I'm going to be a cripple for the rest of my life?"

"Don't jump to any conclusions. All I can say is that you're suffering from a serious illness we don't know much about yet. I'm going to write a prescription. If that doesn't help in a few days, we can discuss the possibility of an operation."

"The possibility of an operation? Which means

you're not sure it will succeed, right?"

"I'll do my best, but I can't promise anything. In any case, surgery may not be necessary."

The diagnosis left him completely stunned. And when a nurse came in to help him try out his "new" wheelchair, he almost broke down. He couldn't believe it. This was no joke! Here he was, sitting in a wheelchair, for God's sake! He was overcome with anxiety, as if he'd just been told he had only a couple of months to live. He broke out in a cold sweat and felt like shouting that it wasn't true, that it was all just a bad dream.

But he was soon forced to come to terms with the reality of his situation as the nurse pushed him out into the corridor and another patient, who had been in a wheelchair for years, saluted him as if John had suddenly become a member of a select "club."

He was discharged that same afternoon and took a cab home. At the door to his apartment he had to wait while the taxi driver got out and helped him into his wheelchair. One of his neighbors saw him and paled, asking what had happened, if he'd had some kind of an accident.

In the elevator John had to answer more questions from another neighbor, so that he was relieved when he finally closed the door to his apartment, accomplished with some difficulty, since he was still unused to getting around in a wheelchair, discovering unexpected obstacles everywhere he turned.

The possibility of such a sudden turn of events had been the farthest thing from his mind when he'd returned from his visit to the old millionaire's mansion, triumphant and assured of his future success. Then he noticed the Tiffany box with the engagement ring he'd bought for Rachel still inside. How in heaven's name was he going to announce the terrible news to her?

CHAPTER 13

In which the young man has to make the most difficult decision of his life . . .

RACHEL KNOCKED on John's door at seven sharp, as planned, just a few minutes after John had hidden his wheelchair away in a cupboard.

"It's open!" he called from the living room sofa, where he'd installed himself, his legs covered with a blanket, dressed in pajamas and slippers, an outfit Rachel found very strange.

Why didn't he get up to greet her, take her in his arms as he usually did? She had on her short, clinging red dress, with its plunging neckline, that had never left John indifferent before.

"I have a touch of the flu," John hurriedly explained as a way of justifying his immobility.

Worried, Rachel walked over to the couch, kissed

him on the cheek, and then placed a maternal hand on his forehead to see if he had any fever. His temperature seemed normal.

Seeing her standing so close, breathing in her intoxicating perfume, John felt like telling her what he'd never dared tell another woman. That not only did he find her beautiful, that the effect she had on him was beyond words, but that she was his reason for living, his one and only love, his anchor, his bread and wine, without whom life was simply a slow journey toward death.

Did she know how much he loved her? Did she know that during his long hours of reflection he'd finally understood, once and for all, that separating from her would be like tearing a part out of himself?

"There's some white wine in the fridge," John said.

"Do you think it's a good idea to drink in your condition?"

"A glass of wine never killed anyone."

"All right, if you say so. . . ."

She didn't feel like arguing and went to the kitchen. In the fridge she found a bottle of very ordinary white wine, but next to it she noticed another bottle, this one an excellent quality champagne—bought by John the day before—which confirmed her suspicion that he had a very important and very felicitous announcement to make. After all, John wasn't the type to buy champagne for nothing; he had obviously decided to celebrate their engagement and would finally give her the beautiful ring she'd seen by chance the night they'd become lovers. She wouldn't hesitate in accepting.

When he saw her return with the bottle of champagne instead of the white wine, John frowned slightly, almost imperceptibly. Rachel, however, noticed the change in his expression—she was almost obsessively attentive to any alterations in his mood. Had he had a sudden change of heart? Maybe he wasn't feeling up to the occasion in his present condition?

"Would you prefer drinking something else?" she asked.

"No, no, why do you say that?"

"No reason. Just a feeling. How about some coffee instead?"

"No, what's the matter with you?" he protested.

She started opening the champagne, but he took the bottle from her hands, popped the cork, and filled the glasses she'd brought and placed on the little end table next to the couch. They both tasted the bubbling elixir, after which Rachel got up and put on some music, not just any music but "their" song, "Unforgettable." Then she came and sat beside him on the couch, raised her glass, and said, "A toast. To . . ."

But she didn't finish, not daring to say "To us," preferring to wait until it came from him. Rachel nervously emptied her glass and poured herself another, while John absently sipped his. She thought he might ask her to dance, despite feeling sick, but instead he said, "I saw Rogers. We didn't get the contract."

"Oh, that's too bad. But it's really no big deal. We'll get others, you'll see. Maybe we should promote the agency some more."

"Listen, Rachel, I have something to tell you. I made a decision, a decision that wasn't easy, believe me. I'm going to close the agency for a while."

"Close the agency! But why? We're . . . we're still doing okay, at least we were the last time I checked our bank statement."

"I know but . . . this is a personal decision. I want to do something else with my life."

"Write a screenplay?"

"Yes."

"I see."

John took an envelope from the end table and, looking extremely embarrassed, added, "I wrote you a check for a month's salary. That should give you enough time to find something else. If you need a letter of recommendation, of course, I'd be . . ."

This time she felt it really was the end. John hadn't

acted like part of a couple when he'd made his decision. He hadn't bothered to consult her at all. Sure, the agency belonged to him, he could do whatever he wanted with it, but after all, they'd been lovers for months now, and she thought she was a part of his life. He handed her the envelope, but she didn't open it. There was a lump in her throat, and she had the feeling that the worst was still to come.

"Don't you think your decision is a little hasty?" she said, thinking that maybe he'd suffered a mild burnout, that he was getting depressed, although she found that somewhat surprising, considering that only a couple of days before he'd been brimming with energy and enthusiasm.

"I have to tell you that . . . I've been thinking a lot about us . . . and I've come to the conclusion that we're really not meant for each other, that it's better if we don't see each other anymore."

Not only was he not asking her to marry him, he was firing her and dumping her at the same time! She felt her world falling apart. He didn't want her anymore! He didn't love her.

Maybe he'd never loved her, but had just used her. It was all so unexpected, so upsetting and humiliating, that Rachel felt she would lose her mind if she stayed and demanded an explanation, which under any other circumstances she would naturally have a right to do. Their love, which she'd found so noble, so romantic, suddenly appeared sordid, just another banal affair between an assistant and her boss, now coming to an abrupt end. She'd been duped.

She felt like shouting and crying at the same time. But she said nothing, silenced by her suffering. Anyway, what good would it do? The verdict he had pronounced on their love was the result of something much bigger than John. It was her destiny, a kind of evil spell hanging over her as far back as she could remember, always arranging her life so that she got involved with men who left her just when she began loving them.

"I understand" was all she said. "I . . . I think I'll go now. You need to rest. . . ."

John was waiting for her to protest, to scream at him and call him all kinds of names or to beg him not to leave her.

"I'll come by the agency tomorrow and pick up my things," she said hoarsely. "I can leave the key with the janitor."

And with those words, without a kiss or even a good-bye, she left, almost running out the door to avoid breaking down in anguish.

As soon as she'd closed the door behind her John struggled off the couch, made his way as best he could to the cupboard where he'd hidden his wheelchair, and climbed back into it. He wheeled himself over to the stereo and played "Unforgettable" again, then hurried to the window and watched Rachel cross the street and stand at the corner, waiting for her bus.

The music reminded him of how they'd danced together at the Plaza Hotel, light as only lovers can be, on their first night out together. Now it was over; it was his fault, his decision. But could he really have done anything else? He would never have accepted her staying with him out of pity. Could he have lived with himself, knowing that he was imposing a life of suffering on the woman he loved, demanding that she become his nursemaid instead of a real wife, pushing his wheelchair around for the rest of her life?

When he saw Rachel get on the bus that carried her off into the night, he hurriedly reached for the little Tiffany box in his pocket, opened it, and contemplated the beautiful ring he'd bought. Tears filled his eyes as he realized he'd just made the most difficult decision of his life and that, any way you looked at it, he had to come out a loser. If he'd kept her, if he'd told her the truth about his illness, he would have lost his self-respect. By letting her go, he'd lost his love.

His condition did not improve the following week, and John, heartbroken, closed down the agency. He negotiated a settlement with the owner of the building. Although the man didn't want to be unreasonable with someone in a wheelchair, business was business, and he demanded three months' rent in exchange for breaking the lease. Another few thousand dollars down the drain!

John put his few belongings into a box—a few pads of unused paper, pens, the portraits of Rachel and of his father, which he'd always kept on his desk. Before leaving, he took a last look around to make sure he hadn't forgotten anything. He opened a drawer in Rachel's desk. Inside he found two paychecks that she'd never cashed, knowing that the agency was having more and more serious financial problems. She'd tried to do her bit, out of love for him and because she was so generous by nature, even though she was poor herself.

John felt ashamed when he realized how much of a sacrifice she'd made. He took the checks and, overcome with emotion, put them in his pocket as carefully as if they'd been love letters.

He was about to close the drawer when he noticed a gold brooch in the form of a little ram, the symbol of Rachel's astrological sign, Aries, her birthday being the first of April. She'd worn it the first day she appeared at the agency, applying for the assistant's job. John picked up the brooch and looked at it for a few seconds. Then, fighting his melancholy, he tried to pin the brooch to his shirt, but clumsily stuck himself with the pin instead, causing a tiny stain of blood to spread over his heart.

Chapter 14

*In which the young
man has to choose
between light and
darkness . . .*

◈

Around five o'clock the next morning John was driven by taxi to the shore of the East River, near the Brooklyn Bridge. He asked the driver to wait, a request the man found somewhat strange. Nevertheless he got out of his car, leaned back against the door, and lit up a cigarette, looking tired.

Propped in his wheelchair, John found himself just a few feet from the end of a cement dock that rose about twenty yards above the surface of the muddy water. He'd brought along the old wooden box the millionaire had given him, and he looked at it with disgust.

Everything the old man had told him was false, just a bunch of lies and fantastic promises. Sure, he'd been told to expect his share of trials and tribulations, but this descent into hell was just too much. His life was supposed to have been a garden of roses, bringing him one success after another. But when he took stock of his real situation, things didn't look all that rosy.

He'd had to close down his agency; he'd lost Rachel, the woman he loved most in his life; he was paralyzed, confined to a wheelchair, without knowing if he'd ever regain the use of his legs.

Why go on? For whom? If only his father were still alive . . . How often he'd told himself that he should have accepted his father's repeated offers to come and work in the bar. Had he done so, his life could have been completely different. Maybe he wouldn't have been stricken with this strange disease. On the other hand, he wouldn't have met Rachel either, which, upon reflection, might have been preferable. Because isn't it better never to experience great love than to be condemned to keep on living after you lose it?

He looked at the old box in turmoil, then advanced toward the end of the dock. The taxi driver, seeing how close he was to the edge, dropped his cigarette in alarm and took a few steps forward. What was this guy up to? Was he about to commit the ultimate act and throw himself into the turbulent water below? And if so, who would pay for the ride?

His fears dissolved as John threw the old box into the

river instead of himself. He watched it float away on the current until it sank and disappeared.

John felt like following the box to its watery grave. It was like a deep, mysterious calling, a call to silence, to calm, to the end of all suffering. It would be simple, so simple. All he had to do was give the wheels of his chair a little shove and he'd rejoin his father, ask for his forgiveness for refusing to work alongside him at his bar. Who did he think he was, turning down his father's request? He wouldn't have to think about Rachel either; he wouldn't have to regret leaving her anymore because there was nothing else he could have done. As if in a trance, he placed his right hand on the wheel, ready to make the final gesture, and stared down at the water.

John was still struggling with his desire to end it all when the first rays of the sun flashed up over the horizon and reflected across the waves, filling him with great emotion. The orange light of dawn, spreading across the clear blue sky, was so incredibly beautiful that briefly he thought he heard a single word—"om,".

But at the very last moment, as if his strength suddenly deserted him—or, rather, as if a strange force had suddenly taken possession of him, stripping him of his will to die—at that moment he had a vision: the sick rosebush in the millionaire's garden leaped into his mind, and a voice sounded within him, very faintly at first, a voice that sounded just like the old eccentric saying, "The only reason I came back was for this rosebush."

His resolution began to weaken as he realized that he couldn't do this to the old millionaire, that the rosebush that was almost dead was himself.

And suddenly he found he wanted to live, because someone had touched him in a way beyond words, beyond all material things. . . . And despite everything, he believed in that man, despite his strange ways, and despite the mysterious, inexplicable side to his teachings. More important, he realized, this man believed in him.

What! Did he take himself that seriously, attach so much importance to his own little person that he was ready to kill himself, even though he was still able to marvel at this grand spectacle of nature and feel moved by it? Was he so obsessed with his own unhappiness that he couldn't see the extraordinary beauty of life right there before his eyes?

He recalled what the old man had said when they were riding in his limousine and he'd pointed to an ill-dressed man standing on the curb: the difference between that man and himself was that even if you took away everything the millionaire owned, he'd sooner or later get it all back, because he still had the most important thing a person can possess—his mind.

He'd lost the use of his legs; he'd lost Rachel, his father, the agency . . . everything. But he still had his mind. It was intact. And it was because of his mind that he could still appreciate the splendor of a Manhattan sunrise, creating a surreal landscape of skyscrapers and painted sky before him.

His mind was his greatest source of wealth. And he was going to use it to fight, to make his dreams come true. He'd write the screenplay that would change his life once and for all.

"In the greatest adversity," the old man had explained, "lies the seed of highest achievement." At the time John had not known what that achievement would be. But now he was ready, ready to make an act of faith in life, in his future success. It was time he act on his dream.

CHAPTER 15

In which the young man resolutely sets to work . . .

LESS THAN half an hour later John was seated at his desk in front of his computer, which would likely be his only companion for the next few weeks. He immediately concluded that the simplest—and therefore the most interesting—story he had to tell was the one about his meeting with the extraordinary old millionaire. He'd never written a screenplay, but his long experience as an advertising writer had sharpened his skill with words and developed his already fertile imagination.

He'd hardly been working a few minutes when a blue jay came along and perched on the ledge of the open window next to his desk. It was the first time he'd seen a blue jay in New York. Excited at seeing his favorite bird again, he hurried to the kitchen for some nuts and threw a few onto the ledge. The jay pecked at the largest one, picking it up in its black beak, and flew off. John remembered the recurring dream he'd had about a wingless blue jay and immediately concluded that this blue jay's visit was a good omen. A new life was beginning for him, despite adversity, despite the pain of losing Rachel. He had to throw himself into his work, body and soul. He had to concentrate with all of his power.

His years in advertising had prepared him for work under pressure, so he was able to put in double shifts, spending fifteen hours a day, seven days a week, in front of the computer. At this rate he was able to complete a first draft in a month.

The first thing he did was pay a visit to his local video store, freshly printed script in hand, to see Steve, one of the employees and an obsessive movie buff, with whom he'd spent long hours discussing the merits and failings of various movies. He'd had occasion to see Steve on a regular basis since meeting Rachel, as their favorite pastime had consisted of watching old classics and eating pizza, half vegetarian, half combination, to satisfy their respective tastes.

"What happened to you?" asked Steve at the video store, seeing John in his wheelchair for the first time.

"I fell getting out of my private jet."

Steve, a twenty-five-year-old film student, hair tied up in a ponytail, with small twinkling eyes, said, "No, seriously, what happened?"

"I don't really know. It's some kind of bizarre disease. Something to do with my spine."

"How long's it going to take before you're better?"

"The doctor doesn't even know that."

"That's a bummer." Then, after a pause, "I hope you didn't contaminate Rachel?"

"No, it's not contagious."

"How is she?"

"She's okay. . . ."

It was as if he felt ashamed to admit that it was over between them, as if allowing their relationship to exist in the mind of someone else somehow kept it alive.

"You really picked a good woman there," Steve continued. "You should marry her before some shark comes along and steals her."

"That's true," said John.

"So what are you renting today?"

"Nothing. I came by to ask you to read my script."

The next day Steve called to tell John what he thought about it. John listened intently.

"Do you want me to tell you what'll make you happy or what I really think?" Steve began.

"I get the feeling I'm in for a rough ride."

"I find it lacks life. I don't believe in the characters. You didn't write this from the heart. Maybe I'm wrong. In Hollywood they say that nobody knows nothing about nothing. So I may be missing the point completely here. The best thing would be to get someone else to read it."

"Thanks."

"I hope I wasn't too heavy on you. I mean, you did ask for my opinion. Maybe I'm too critical. I read about three scripts a day at film school, so I may be a little jaded."

And so John discovered the "joys" of creation. He didn't dare let anyone else read the screenplay. Instead he reread it himself and found that Steve's judgment had been correct. The story lacked life, warmth. He'd written it from his head, not from his heart.

He grew discouraged. After all, who did he think he was? He'd never studied filmmaking, hadn't read a single book on the subject, and here he was thinking he could become a screenwriter overnight. What did he expect?

His conversation with Steve had fired his desire to see Rachel again. Why not call her now and tell her the truth, that he'd never stopped loving her, that he'd lied to her? Maybe she'd understand and come back to him?

Maybe it wasn't too late? After all, they'd been separated for less than a month.

After long hesitation he picked up the phone and dialed her number. But after two rings he suddenly lost courage and hung up. He dialed again, this time letting it ring three times. Trembling, he finally heard Rachel's voice, so beautiful it had never ceased to resonate painfully in his memory.

"Hello?" she said.

". . ."

"Hello? Who is this? Can you hear me?"

John still couldn't say anything, suddenly overcome with shyness.

"Louis? Is that you?" Rachel asked. "Stop joking around, it isn't funny."

John felt a stab in his heart and hung up. Who was this Louis? Could Rachel have already found someone else, after only a month? Maybe Steve's warning at the video club had been prophetic. A "shark" had come along and stolen Rachel because he hadn't asked her to marry him in time. No, he thought, it wasn't possible.

Rachel was much too sensitive and romantic to forget so quickly, after only a few short weeks. Louis was probably just an acquaintance, an old friend at most. Unless her pain and confusion had been so great she'd thrown herself into the arms of the first person who came along.

Hoping to get his mind off Rachel, John turned on the TV. A beautiful woman was advertising vacation spots in Acapulco. John immediately thought of Rachel.

Why not call her and invite her to take a week off with him in order to straighten things out?

Chapter 16

*In which the young
man experiences
humiliation . . .*

JOHN WAS on the beach, sitting in his wheelchair admiring Rachel's gracious curves. Wearing a clinging black one-piece bathing suit with pretty apple-green buttons on the shoulder straps, she was splashing around in the perfectly still waters of Acapulco Bay. How beautiful she was, with her chestnut curls falling from under a yellow straw hat like golden rays. How luminous her smile was, how guileless and innocent, like a child's.

There was a festive atmosphere on the crowded beach. Behind the spot Rachel and John had chosen to place their towels a mariachi band, hired by their hotel, the Acapulco Plaza, sent a stream of joyous guitar and trumpet melodies up toward the perfectly azure sky.

The only blemish on this idyllic tableau was John's neighbor, an enormous man in his forties who had surely broken a few scales in his day—he must have weighed over three hundred and fifty pounds! To top it off, he was clad in a ridiculous little leopard-skin bathing suit, with folds of flab falling out like layers of icing. He was asleep now, after devouring a gigantic plate of spaghetti. The leftovers lay discarded by his side, attracting a horde of flies.

But the worst of it was that he'd fallen asleep before finishing his dessert, an enormous strawberry sundae, which had fallen onto his prodigious belly, where it lay melting in the midday sun, sending rivers of ice cream flowing down between his flabby thighs and drawing even more flies to the immediate vicinity. John, bothered by the insects, and finding it very difficult to move his wheelchair in the soft sand, cleared his throat a few times, hoping to wake the man up. The grotesque spectacle soon became the center of attraction on that part of the beach. John tried coughing, and when that didn't work, either, he leaned over and grabbed hold of the knife on the man's plate of spaghetti, a fairly long knife, and began using it to bang on the metal part of the wheels of his chair, a tactic that proved just as futile and that John suddenly abandoned as he looked once again at Rachel and saw something that sent a chill running through him: an enormous shark fin was cutting through the waters of the bay, heading for Rachel, who was one of only a few bathers at that hour.

"Rachel! Get back to shore! Rachel! There's a shark behind you!" he screamed, waving wildly with his arms.

Rachel didn't hear him because the music of the orchestra drowned out his cries. She must have thought he was waving to encourage her, or to show her how happy he was, and waved back, smiling happily.

John realized she couldn't hear him and that he had to do something right away. He tried to alert the people around him, but those who were stretched out on the sand all seemed to be asleep, while the only couple who were awake understood only Spanish, a language John could hardly speak.

"Rachel! Behind you!"

The shark was only about a hundred yards off, heading straight for her. John knew he had to act right away. He remembered what the old man had told him, that faith could accomplish anything. If it could move mountains, it could also shake the paralysis out of his legs and get him out of his wheelchair so that he could rush to the aid of his beloved in distress.

He gripped the armrests of the chair, concentrated, and tried to get up, repeating in his mind that he *could* walk, he *had* to walk, Rachel's life depended on it. And the miracle happened. He pushed off the armrests and, to his own surprise, as if regaining his strength was the last thing he'd expected to happen, he didn't fall. With the fat man's knife still in his hand, John began running, slowly at first, and then more and more rapidly, shouting to Rachel to get out of the water. He brandished the knife over his head in such a menacing fashion that Rachel, at first surprised and happy to see him so miraculously recovered, began wondering if he'd been out in the sun too long. What was he trying to do, running toward her through the surf, waving a knife over his head?

She soon thought he'd lost his mind completely as, instinctively raising a hand to protect herself, she watched him leap into the air and fling himself behind her, just as the shark was about to attack her. A long struggle ensued, which she watched in terror.

John disappeared below the surface, engaged in mortal combat with a shark that weighed over two hundred pounds. The water soon turned crimson, blood seemed to spurt from everywhere and nowhere at once. Then the water grew suddenly calm and a dead body floated to the surface, the shark's, riddled with knife wounds. John reappeared, gasping for breath, on the point of suffocating. He didn't seem to have suffered any wounds.

He looked around for Rachel but she was nowhere to be seen. To his horror he noticed her straw hat floating on the surface of the water.

"Rachel!" he screamed desperately, almost in a panic, imagining the worst. And yet he'd gotten to the shark before it'd had a chance to attack. He looked back at the beach—maybe she'd headed for shore in fear when she realized there was a shark in the water. But she was nowhere in sight. He dove down, searching under water. Nothing. He returned to the surface and looked out to sea, and then he saw it—a second shark fin speeding away from the site of the combat. It seemed that another predator had carried Rachel off during the struggle.

John's despair was boundless. He immediately blamed himself for not having seen the second shark. But even if he had, could he have fought off two sharks at the same time? This was destiny, striking cruelly once again. He moaned in pain, retrieved Rachel's hat, and, shoulders bowed, began wading through the surf toward the beach.

An attractive young woman stood waiting for him on the beach, her lovely lips parted in an admiring smile. She'd seen him attack the shark, although she had no idea that another monster of the depths had carried Rachel off. She pointed to the floating corpse of the dead shark, already being picked at by a flock of gulls.

"I saw the whole thing," she said. "You're so brave. Can I get you a drink?"

John didn't answer, but simply glanced at her with derision. When the water level fell to his knees, he suddenly felt his legs giving way beneath him. He soon realized what was happening—his strength had lasted only long enough for him to try to save Rachel. Now that it was over he'd lose it again. He could concentrate as hard as he liked, it wouldn't do any good. He soon crumpled into the shallow water, tried desperately to get up, but in vain.

The girl frowned, wondering what was going on, then saw the empty wheelchair on the beach and understood.

"You're handicapped," she said.

And she burst out laughing, calling her friends over, most of whom were athletic types with muscles swollen from hours of pumping iron and a steady diet of steroids.

"Look at this," she squealed. "The guy's a cripple but he can swim! And to think I just offered to buy him a drink. I don't drink with cripples, no sir, not me!"

They all started laughing uproariously while John, completely stunned by the pain of losing Rachel, kept trying to get up, flailing his arms in the water to distance himself from the cruel vacationers. Then the wail of a police siren sounded and they all dispersed.

And that's how John's nightmare ended; he woke up, alone in his bed, with the vacation section of the newspaper on the floor beside him, open to a page advertising the irresistible charms of the Acapulco Plaza hotel. Outside his bedroom window the sound of a police siren wailed in the distance, obviously the one that had pulled him from his troubled sleep.

His body bathed in sweat, as if he had really been engaged in some exhausting combat, John took a few deep breaths, immensely relieved that it had all been just a bad dream, that he hadn't really lost Rachel forever. And yet it had all seemed so real; he'd experienced it all with such hallucinating clarity: the beach, the fat man next to him, Rachel, divine in her black bathing suit, and the shark he'd fought with . . .

He wondered what time it could be and checked his watch—five past seven in the morning. At least he could have a good cup of coffee. And as the police siren faded into the distance, John made a move to stand up, also having forgotten that he couldn't walk, and fell flat on his face, at once ashamed and discouraged that his legs, so strong in the past, were now useless, like a pair of old rags.

He pulled himself up with great difficulty and sat on the edge of his bed. He reached for his daily dose of medication but, suddenly disgusted at the pills' apparent inability to improve his condition, threw the open container away, sending a score of red-and-black capsules rolling across the floor.

Then he recalled a part of his dream, and his face lit up with hope. On the beach, during the emergency, he had summoned up all his inner force, all the power of his faith, and had *miraculously succeeded in getting up and walking.* Why couldn't he do the same thing while awake? Can't the things we experience in dreams be repeated in real life? Is what we mistakenly refer to as "real life" so very different from the life we lead in our dreams? In any case, it was worth a try.

He began concentrating, as he had in the dream, repeating over and over that he could do it if only he could *really believe,* then stood up. For an instant he thought the miracle was actually happening again, that he had regained the use of his legs. But his elation lasted for only a fraction of a second, time enough for his face to light up with a triumphant smile and then darken just as quickly as the sad reality of his condition once again became apparent. He fell again.

He sat there for a few minutes, thinking about Rachel, about her life, which surely wasn't easy despite her eternal optimism. He missed her more than ever—rarely had he felt so alone.

Three hours later, at his weekly appointment at the hospital to see Dr. Grant, the nurse asked him to change into a hospital gown and stretch out on the examining table, which he did.

As soon as she left the room Dr. Grant walked in and offered his large hand in greeting.

"How are you today, Mr. Blake?"

"Oh, just wonderful," John replied.

"No."

"Oh, I'm getting better and better day by day, Doctor. I signed up for the Boston marathon, and I'm planning to finish in first place. I'll just have to make sure to oil my wheelchair. It's getting a little rusty."

"No improvement?"

"None."

"But you're not getting any worse, either, are you?"

"When something is dead, can it get *more* dead?"

"No, but . . ."

"Why don't you operate, Doctor?"

"An operation would be risky."

"It would be even riskier if I died of boredom."

"First we have to see if the medication is working."

"It isn't. You can see that for yourself."

"You have to be patient. In a few months maybe . . ."

A few months! John could hardly imagine waiting a few months, when each day that went by was torture. He didn't argue further, but when the examination was over and he left the hospital he felt even more discouraged than when he'd first found out he was ill.

CHAPTER 17

*In which
the young man
discovers eternal
life . . .*

WHEN HE left the hospital John hailed a taxi and told the driver to take him to the cemetery where his father was buried. He made a brief stop along the way to buy a bottle of the best cognac and a small bouquet of flowers.

As they drove through the iron gates leading into the cemetery John recalled his father's burial service, attended by a few family members whom he hardly ever saw—distant cousins, an old aunt and uncle—as well as a few regulars from the bar and his father's faithful helper, Madeline, the only person, aside from John, who had really been saddened by his father's death—in any case, the only one to shed any tears. The priest, visibly tipsy, had been in a hurry to get the service over with before the impending storm broke. He speeded things up as best he could, to the relief of the mourners, who distractedly made the sign of the cross and dispersed as the first peals of thunder resounded in the overcast sky.

John remembered the gravediggers throwing the first clods of earth onto his father's coffin, swearing with the effort (the earth being heavy with the previous day's rain), also in a hurry to finish before the storm broke.

With a heavy heart John had told himself that a man's life really didn't mean much when even his loved ones forgot so quickly, especially when their own comfort happened to be threatened by a few drops of water.

But the service had done its job—the physical reality of seeing his father's coffin lifted and placed into the gaping hole in the ground had finally made John realize that it was over, that he'd never see his father again. And curiously, although he'd had a family for over thirty years, he suddenly felt like an orphan.

He found his father's tombstone, a small, very modest affair, placed next to his mother's, which gave rise to the consoling thought that at least his mother and father, inseparable during their lifetimes, were, in a manner of speaking, together again.

He laid the little bouquet of flowers on his father's grave but then, deciding that he was demonstrating a lack of respect, or at least of tenderness, for his dear departed mother, split the bouquet in two and placed half on her grave.

"Hi, Dad," he said out loud. "I hope you're okay. I'm doing just great. As you can see, I'm rolling right along. Oh, all right, I'm in a wheelchair, maybe I'll be paralyzed for the rest of my life, and Rachel and I are separated . . . you know how it is, after a few months you get tired of the routine, and there are so many other women running after me. Good thing I have a fast wheelchair! I've been thinking about putting in a motor, a little turbo job so I can impress my fans and all the photographers chasing after me all the time. . . .

"As for my work, things couldn't be better. I had to close the agency because there was so much to do I didn't have time to write my screenplays, what with all those Hollywood producers breaking down the door to sign contracts and advance me thousands of dollars. So as you can see, life is beautiful, and I thought I'd come and celebrate with you."

He pulled the bottle of cognac and a little plastic cup from his pocket, filled the cup to the brim, and raised it high in the air.

"To your health, Dad, wherever you may be!"

He emptied the cup in a single gulp and threw it aside distractedly. He was about to discard the half-empty bottle as well, then changed his mind as he had a rather bizarre idea. He glanced around to see if there were any other visitors in the cemetery, then thought, "What the hell, even if there are, I'm alone here with my father, alone in the world." He wheeled his chair closer to the tombstone and reached out to touch it, with some apprehension, as if death could somehow be contagious. He quickly got used to the smooth cold contact of the stone and, with his other hand, poured the rest of the cognac over his father's tombstone, as if performing a baptismal rite.

"There you go, Dad. I know you would have enjoyed that, even though it's on the rocks, and no one drinks cognac on the rocks, especially not you."

He laughed nervously, then shed a tear as all the pain he had been suppressing for months rose up inside him all at once, drowning him.

A strange scene came to mind, something that had happened during his stay at the old millionaire's mansion. During a conversation they'd had over dinner, as the millionaire was trying to explain that life was perfect, that everything that happened was for the best, John had protested that his father had left this world too soon.

"Too soon for whom?" the old man asked.

"For me," John said, a little confused.

"He left right on time. Every being is assigned a pre-

cise moment to leave this sphere of existence, even before they are born. He accomplished what he had to do
here and was expected elsewhere, to begin a new stage
of his life. You'll have the opportunity to meet him
again, in nine years—"

"In nine years?" John asked, intrigued.

He immediately thought that the old man meant he
would die in nine years, since that would be the only
way of rejoining his father.

"You'll show him his tie . . ."

John brought a hand up to his tie, the same one he'd
taken from his father just after his death. It was the second time the eccentric gardener had alluded to the tie,
the first being when he'd met John at the café terrace
and mentioned how much he admired it. Had he
guessed that the tie had belonged to John's departed father? He hadn't had time to ask, as the millionaire said,
"Follow me, I want to show you something."

He led him to the magnificent main stairway and
stopped in front of the portrait of Jesus, saying, "Just as
the King of Kings said that there are many rooms in his
Father's house, so your life, and that of your father, are
only instants of your real life. You don't realize it because you are asleep. That's why sages throughout history have been telling people to wake up. 'Awake and
pray,' Jesus said. When ordinary people take on a new

body, their guides make them forget their past lives so that they will not be troubled in their new incarnation.

"But some persons can remember everything they have been, everything they've experienced. They also know that life is eternal, that ten or twenty years are nothing in terms of real life, and that knowledge gives them infinite patience. They don't judge time in the same way as ordinary people, who become discouraged at the first sign of trouble and can't stand waiting even a year, not to mention five or even twenty years, to harvest the fruits of their efforts.

"Superior persons act with the inner certitude that not only do they have their whole life before them, but dozens of future lives as well. That is why some geniuses reveal their talents at such an early age. In fact, they have been preparing for their present incarnation in their past life, and sometimes over a number of past lives.

"And more than that," the old man continued, "highly evolved persons are endowed with great patience and live each day with a kind of detachment, like an actor who does not confuse his real personality with the role he is playing, because he knows that the ultimate goal of all he does is to transform himself, to perfect his inner self, so that even if he doesn't appear to harvest the fruits of his labors in this lifetime, he is harvesting them all the same, because his nature is transformed. Alchemists may seem to be working on the exterior transformation of lead into gold, but their real work is the transformation of the soul, the transition from old to new.

"This enlightened knowledge gives them freedom and removes all fear of death. Accomplishing each day what they must accomplish, not caring about rewards for their actions even though they may apply themselves heart and soul, they are ready to depart at any moment, any day, if their mission, which is basically always the same—the transformation of their own being and helping others to transform themselves as well—must be carried out elsewhere, with other companions. Because real life is vast, ten thousand times vaster than any conception of it you may presently have."

He fell silent and led John over to a set of huge double doors, painted in white and gold, which he opened, revealing a large, completely empty room, no furniture, no carpets, lit by an immense circular skylight, actually a glass dome decorated with stained glass depicting different varieties of roses.

The two men crossed the room and the millionaire stopped in front of a massive black door, its gold handle sculpted in the form of a snake biting its own tail, the alchemical symbol of accomplishment, self-contentment, and a return to the celestial dwelling that resides, often forgotten, in the hearts of all human beings.

The millionaire turned the handle, pushed the door open, and allowed John to enter what appeared to be an immense wardrobe, more like a kind of walk-in closet. John timidly stepped inside and, to his great surprise, recognized his own clothes.

He touched a jacket, an old navy blue jacket with gold buttons, and recognized it as his own. He'd stopped wearing it about a year before because it was threadbare, practically worn out from use. One of John's habits, practically an obsession with him, and due in part to the fact that he spent so much money eating in restaurants, was to become maniacally attached to his clothes, much like other people become attached to their dogs, so that he stopped wearing them only when absolutely necessary.

A shiver ran down his spine, as invariably happens when people are faced with a phenomenon that is not only strange but that lifts a veil, revealing what we really are, giving us a momentary glimpse of that troubling, although essential, aspect of our being that we so flippantly neglect because it isn't fashionable—an awareness of our own soul.

How did his old jacket happen to be there? Another mystery he couldn't explain. But everything in that house was strange. And there were more surprises to come as, behind the jacket, he saw another, this one brown suede, which he'd loved wearing when he was sixteen years old.

He fell into a kind of trance as he discovered the suit he'd worn to his First Communion, and behind it a pair of pajamas his mother had made for his first birthday and that he recognized from photographs he'd seen of himself at that age.

He found more clothes that he didn't recognize, and that seemed much older, as if they'd belonged to his father when he'd been young—although John didn't know much about fashion, he figured they came from the twenties. Then he saw a Renaissance-style page's uniform, bright red, next to which hung a heavy brown cassock that seemed to have belonged to a Franciscan monk of the Middle Ages.

This was followed by a succession of clothes from almost every century, almost like a crash course in the history of fashion throughout the ages. The collection ended with a beautiful white linen tunic that seemed to go back to the time of Christ.

John, still in a daze, and having no idea what all this was about—although a part of him could guess—turned to the old millionaire for an explanation, or at least a hint of what the cupboard and its contents meant.

Then the old millionaire said something that sent a shock of insight, a golden ray of true understanding, through John's being.

"You have worn all these clothes."

CHAPTER 18

*In which
the young man
discovers the power
of having a goal . . .*

JOHN COULD find no better way of consoling himself, of forgetting his cares, than to throw himself back into his work. In a month he completed a new version of his screenplay. Unfortunately, Steve, the video store employee who had been so severe in his judgment of the initial attempt, didn't like the second draft, either, which deeply undermined John's confidence.

Decidedly he had embarked on something that was much more difficult than he'd thought. It had been presumptuous of him to believe that he could just sit down and become a screenwriter, like someone who thinks he is a mathematician just because he can add up his grocery bill! He felt like giving up, returning to the Gladstone Agency and asking for his job back. After all, he'd been a brilliant and loyal employee of the firm for years.

Of course, he hadn't resigned under the best of circumstances, leaving without notice and causing his boss to lose an important client. But there was always a chance that Gladstone might have already forgotten the incident and would be ready to wipe the slate clean. John had done some personal accounting and found his finances in dire straits.

By tightening his belt he could last for three or four months, five at most, and he experienced a kind of fear that he had never known as a regularly paid employee, that of literally dying of hunger, of being evicted from his apartment because he wouldn't be able to pay the rent, and worst of all, of losing his beloved Mustang.

But then he recalled the boredom and the agony he'd felt working at the Gladstone Agency, and he told himself that he would do everything possible to avoid going back. Writing a decent screenplay couldn't be as difficult as all that! He'd read a lot of stories about people who'd succeeded on their first attempt, like the Los Angeles waitress who had managed to sell her first script to Michael Douglas for two hundred and fifty thousand dollars. It eventually became the box office smash *Romancing the Stone.*

So it was possible. He supposed he just wasn't going about it the right way. Comfortably seated on his fa-

vorite couch, an antique he'd bought at a secondhand
store, he was meditating on these questions, surrounded by the scattered pages of his second draft,
which he'd tossed aside in discouragement. He recalled
the amazing scene that had taken place at the millionaire's mansion, when he'd spoken about the importance
of setting goals.

The two men had been on the beach that bordered
one end of the millionaire's rose garden.

"How much money do you plan on making with
your first screenplay?"

"I don't know," John said, finding the question very
matter-of-fact.

"That's a mistake."

"How can I know how much I'll make if I have to sell
it first?"

"You'll never achieve anything of greatness with that
approach. You have to start by setting yourself a precise
goal—in this case, a specific amount of money. Then
you put your inner forces to work and let your mind
guide you. Before leaving on a trip you make plans, you
decide on a destination. If not, you'll end up anywhere,
usually not where you want to go. So tell me, how much
are you planning to earn by selling your first screenplay?"

"I don't know. Ten thousand dollars maybe?"

The millionaire burst out laughing.

"We really have a lot of work to do with you. Make an effort. Let's have a more substantial figure."

"I don't know. How about twenty-five thousand?"

"Come on, don't be afraid to think big. Do you want to become a millionaire or not?"

"A hundred thousand dollars?"

"Well, that's a little better. But why not two hundred and fifty thousand?"

"All right, two hundred and fifty thousand."

"Do you really think you can earn that much?"

"Yes, well, what I mean is . . . I know it isn't impossible, since some people have been paid that much for their first screenplay, sometimes even more."

"And how long do you plan to spend writing this screenplay?"

"I hadn't thought about it. Is it really that important? Inspiration is a tricky thing. A screenplay isn't something you write in a few weeks. You have to let the story ripen awhile."

Once again the gardener broke into his inimitable laughter. He sounded like a teenager who'd just heard the funniest joke in the world.

"You really have a great sense of humor," he said when his sparkling laugh finally died down. He paused, thought for a moment, and then said, "I'm going to make a bet with you."

"A bet?"

"Yes. You see that umbrella down there?" he said, pointing to a blue-and-gold beach umbrella about two hundred yards down the beach, protecting an elderly couple from the rays of the sun.

"Yes."

"I bet I can reach it faster than you can."

"You want to race with me?"

"Exactly."

"But I . . . I mean, I respect you a lot but, well, I'm much younger than you are and . . ."

"I didn't ask how old you were, I asked if you want to bet. You're afraid of losing, is that it?"

"No," John replied indignantly. "Listen, if you really want to do this—"

"All right, how much do we bet? A thousand dollars?"

John swallowed hard. He hadn't expected the wager to be so much. But he was in the company of a millionaire, and as the saying goes, when in Rome . . .

"Okay, sure," he said.

The millionaire led him to a little beach cabin, gaily painted in red and white, where visitors could change into their bathing costumes. It contained a number of life jackets, Windsurfers, oars, umbrellas, and so on, everything his guests needed to have fun on the beach. He opened the door, which had no padlock, and pulled out a pair of long stilts, which he then mounted with surprising agility for a man his age. Before doing so, he rolled his trousers up to his thighs, revealing his fine muscular legs, with not an ounce of fat on them, or any bulging veins—in fact, completely devoid of any of the natural signs of aging.

"I'm ready," he declared.

"But . . . I didn't think . . ." John began to protest as he realized that the old gardener intended to use the stilts for the race. But he changed his mind. With or without stilts, no seventy-year-old was going to beat a man of his age, in the prime of his physical strength.

"Is there a problem?"

"No, no problem," John said. "Whenever you're ready."

"One, two, three . . . Go!" the millionaire proclaimed gaily.

And he took off, handling the stilts with incredible skill, bounding over the sand as if he were riding a giant compass. At first, taken by surprise, John allowed himself to fall behind, although he was confident he could catch up to the old man without much trouble. He accelerated, and then realized that the millionaire was going faster as well. He was already a dozen yards ahead. What John hadn't accounted for was the softness of the sand—his feet sank in at each step, so that he couldn't get a firm grip, and he found he was spending all his energy just to keep moving, while the millionaire seemed to be flying along the beach. Frustrated and enraged, John tripped and fell. He managed to get back up on his feet and ran as fast as he could, but to no avail—he crossed the finish line, marked by the blue-and-gold parasol, in second place.

Still on his stilts, the millionaire turned to face John, smiling broadly, not in the least out of breath, while John was left gasping for air.

"A thousand dollars," the millionaire said, jumping down off the stilts and placing them over his shoulder. "You owe me a thousand dollars."

"I'm not sure I . . ." John said, looking through his pockets.

"That's okay, you can pay me later."

As they returned to the beach hut to replace the stilts, the millionaire explained: "A goal is like this pair of stilts. It allows a man of my age to win a race against someone as young as you are. Most people only make use of a tiny portion of their true potential. If you have a lofty goal, you can exceed even your own expectations. Remember this in everything you undertake. But don't forget that there are two sides to every goal, just as I could not have won the race with only one stilt. You have to set an amount—*and* a time limit in which to attain it. If you don't, it would be like sitting in a boat in the middle of a lake and rowing with only one oar, always on the same side. You can row with all your strength, and you may have all the good intentions in the world, but you'll still keep going around in circles. You'll just sit there, vegetating. But people who have a clear and precise goal, with an amount they wish to earn and a time limit in which to earn it, even though they may be less gifted than you, less diligent, and less educated, will make steady progress toward their objective, and you'll wonder, as will others, how it is that they have gotten so far ahead of everyone else. This is the magic of having a goal, and the power of those who think big."

He got down on one knee and wrote the amount they'd established for the future sale of John's screenplay in the sand: "$250,000."

"Now you," he said. "Write the amount of time you intend to give yourself to attain your goal."

John thought a moment, and then bent over and wrote "three months."

"No," the millionaire corrected him, "you have to choose a date. A specific date three months from now."

John made a rapid calculation, then erased "three months" and wrote a date instead.

The millionaire looked on in satisfaction, as if John

had just accomplished something really important, then pointed to the sea and said, "Now you have to repeat your goal morning and night, as often as the waves wash up on the sand, because life makes us forget our goals as surely as the wind will erase what we've just written in the sand. That's the best way to make your goal a part of you, to communicate it to your subconscious mind, which in turn, nourished by your commands, will set to work. You will be amazed at the power your inner wisdom will put at your disposal as soon as you give it clear and precise orders."

"I won't forget," John said.

The two men fell silent for a moment. As they turned and gazed out to sea they suddenly heard the cries of what seemed like a teenage girl in distress, out in the water about a hundred yards from shore. Without a moment's hesitation the millionaire leaped into action, followed a second later by John, who was surprised to note that even without stilts the old man had no trouble outrunning him, pumping his powerful legs like an athlete.

He got to the water well ahead of John, splashed through the surf as far as he could, and then dove in and swam toward the drowning girl. He grabbed her from behind and swam forcefully back to shore, where he laid her out on the sand, unconscious. Since she wasn't breathing he immediately started administering emergency first aid, rhythmically pressing down on her chest and then releasing. After a few seconds the girl started coughing and spitting water, until she finally opened her eyes and realized she had been saved.

A few bystanders, among them the girl's parents, were running toward them, but as soon as he saw that he wasn't needed anymore, the millionaire stood up and said to John, "Come on, let's go."

And he jogged off jauntily, rolling his pants legs down along the way. John said nothing and followed, once again admiring his mentor's amazingly powerful, athletic legs.

"You saved her life."

"It is said that when you save one life, you save all humanity. Now, that's something," the millionaire said. "But an even greater thing is to free someone, so that they do not have to return here and die again, which is the way with most people. And by liberating one person, you liberate all humanity. Because once a person is free, his or her immediate, imperative, and unavoidable duty is to free someone else before departing, whose duty, in turn, will be the same, and so on and so on. Throughout all real history, which, as Nietzsche said, is only a series of random paths taken by nature in its quest to create a great human being, there exists a

golden thread, unbroken since time immemorial, transmitted from one initiate to another, that constitutes
real history compared to that other history, which is
just a sad narration of wars and absurd misery."

A question had been bothering John since he'd first
met the old millionaire, and what had just taken place
only added to his curiosity, so that he finally came out
and said, "How old are you exactly, if you don't mind
my asking."

"How old do you think I am?"

"I don't know. If I were to judge by the way you
run . . . I mean, you didn't need those stilts to beat me."

"I placed myself at a disadvantage, not wanting to
humiliate a thirty-year-old like you."

"So, how old are you?"

"You probably won't believe me, but I'm a hundred
and two."

"A hundred and two? That's not possible."

"Among the mountain people I come from I am still
considered a young man. You see, my brothers have discovered the secret of youth. Society fills our heads with
all kinds of false information about age and youth. People are genetically programmed to live to a hundred
and twenty. But we are conditioned to think that a person of sixty is already old, even though he or she should
be in their prime. What makes people age prematurely

is the fact they don't live in the present, nor do they fill their lives with love. People who love all beings, all situations, who don't worry about the future or carry the burden of the past around on their shoulders, such persons do not age in the proper sense of the word. Disease cannot affect them because they live in harmony, and disease is only a message that is sent to us whenever our inner harmony is disturbed by incorrect mental attitudes. Think about it. Try to recall the last day you spent without thinking any negative thoughts, without feeling any hate toward anyone. You have to be vigilant and transform each of those negative thoughts into thoughts of love. Become a child again, welcoming others with open arms, without prejudice, without hate.

"Of course, there are other factors that cause most people to age before their time, such as eating twice as much as they should, breathing ten times less than they should, and allowing their real potential to remain dormant."

The two men passed a group of children who were industriously constructing a castle in the sand. The old man slowed down and observed them. They seemed to be working as a team, some building towers, others trudging back from the shore with buckets of water to fill the moats protecting the castle from imaginary invaders.

"If people fear death more than anything, it is simply because they have never been really happy even once in their lives, not even for an instant. Fear of death arises from this desire to experience real happiness at least once before leaving this Earth. And why are people so unhappy? Because, like these children, they spend their days building castles in the sand, only to be astonished the next morning when they find that the sea has washed the fruit of their labors away. Don't make the same mistake. Turn inward, discover God in your heart and in the hearts of everyone you meet."

When they reached the beach hut, John looked around for the place where he and the millionaire had drawn his goal in the sand. The date John had written down was gone, swept away completely by the wind. But mysteriously, the amount inscribed by the millionaire was still perfectly readable.

CHAPTER 19

*In which
the young man
thinks about the life
he lost . . .*

ALTHOUGH HIS financial resources were rapidly diminishing, John wanted to take a few days off before beginning a new draft of his screenplay. His nervous system was fragile, taxed by the interminable hours of intellectual work he'd put in.

During the period of relative leisure he enjoyed before reassuming the burden of literary creation, he decided that he really had to give up Rachel once and for all, that his indecision and regret were killing him. With a heavy heart he busied himself with a little ritual of rearranging all the little objects on his chest of drawers that reminded him of her, of her love: her portrait, the two checks she'd never cashed, her gold brooch, their engagement ring. He listened to "Unforgettable" a last time, religiously, as if it were a hymn, and then broke the CD.

Eventually he managed to stop thinking about her all that much, surprised at the end of a busy afternoon to realize that two whole hours had passed since he'd thought of her last. He soon believed he was over her, until he got into a taxi and heard Gloria Estefan singing "Here We Are" in her hot, throaty voice, and his heart ripped open again as he saw himself dancing with Rachel to the same song on the terrace of the El Campanario Hotel, with its magnificent mountainside restaurant overlooking Acapulco Bay.

And he understood that he'd been fooling himself, that he hadn't forgotten her, and that he probably never would.

"Where to, buddy?" asked the taxi driver for the second time. He looked in the rearview mirror, saw John's eyes full of tears, and concluded that he must be on some kind of drug.

"Anywhere. Manhattan," John said. "I just want to look around."

On the Brooklyn Bridge the skyscrapers glittering along the New York skyline, a view that usually fascinated him, now left him indifferent. He thought that letting Rachel go had been a terrible mistake. He thought that not only had he lost an extraordinary woman and a sensual and imaginative lover, but also a woman who would have made a perfect mother for his children, which he'd long dreamed of having, and the perfect life partner for himself.

Driving around Manhattan in his taxi, John thought about the emptiness of his present life. He missed Rachel so very much! Everything had been so wonderful when she was around. She added life to everything and everyone she encountered. Because unlike most people he'd met, she lived from the heart and not from her head, although this by no means prevented her from demonstrating her very highly developed intellect.

He made a snap decision, told the taxi driver to go back to Brooklyn, and gave him Rachel's address, instructing him to stop by his place first so he could pick up the engagement ring.

He was firmly resolved to tell her the truth, once and for all. She wouldn't have any trouble believing him, either, since his infirmity was all too obvious. And then he'd ask her, beg her, to take him back, but only on the condition that it wasn't out of pity because he was paralyzed. Maybe with her, through her immense capacity to love, he would recover his health. Hadn't his doctor said that a remission was possible, although he couldn't predict when it would happen, in a month, six months, a year . . .

With Rachel's love he would get through this ordeal much more easily, because wasn't his real unhappiness, his only real hell, being separated from the person he loved most in the world?

He told the taxi driver to stop across the road from her building and wait. His heart was already pounding at the thought of not only talking to Rachel, but of actually seeing her again.

"You know you've got forty-two dollars on the meter already?" the driver said, worried that John might change his mind again and that he might not get paid, although he didn't really expect someone in a wheelchair to make a run for it.

"I'll pay you now," John said, handing the man a fifty-dollar bill.

"That's okay, you don't have to do that," the driver protested, although he could hardly hide his relief.

As John put his wallet back in his pocket he saw Rachel coming out of her building accompanied by a very elegant-looking man in his forties—a lawyer, originally from France, who'd been practicing in New York for a number of years, Louis Renault was his name. He'd been courting Rachel long before she'd met John and had even broken off his engagement to a very rich widow for her sake, although Rachel, largely due to the difference in their ages—he was almost twice as old as

she was—had always politely refused to become intimate with him, offering him her friendship instead.

When John had left her so suddenly, so unexpectedly, Louis Renault had been there for her. He'd offered
his support and had been so caring and gracious that
she'd finally put aside her reservations and accepted his
advances.

John immediately recalled the time he'd called her
on the phone but had been too shy to say anything.
This must be the Louis she'd mentioned, thinking it
was him playing a joke on her.

John couldn't believe it. He felt disgusted, shocked
that the man she'd chosen to replace him was not only
so much older but was obviously very rich as well, if one
could judge by the convertible he was so gallantly helping her climb into.

She hadn't wasted any time, had she, John thought
bitterly. But then he told himself that he was an idiot to
even think like that, that he was the one who'd left her,
with no warning, without any discussion, and not only
that, he'd fired her at the same time, which must have
left her terribly depressed. She had every right to re-
build her life with whomever she thought fit, without
asking for his opinion. Had he asked her what she
thought before leaving her, before firing her? No. Simply put, he'd been the artisan of his own unhappiness,

and now he was reaping the bitter rewards.

Rachel, although she looked a little heavier, had not lost any of her beauty. John watched them get into the car and drive off. Louis Renault turned to her and must have said something funny, because Rachel burst out laughing and put a hand on his shoulder, a gesture that sent another pang through John's heart.

The scene was proof enough that Rachel had begun a new life, that she had gotten over their separation well enough. It suddenly hit him that he'd lost her forever. With a heavy heart John asked the cabdriver to take him home.

CHAPTER 20

In which
the young man
realizes the value of
perseverance . . .

WHEN HE got home, John sadly put the engagement ring back in the drawer where he had placed all his other souvenirs of Rachel, then sat down in front of his rose and began repeating the secret formulations the old gardener had revealed to him. He thought about their conversation on the beach and concluded that one of the reasons he'd failed to write a good screenplay—and an essential condition for selling what he wrote—was that he hadn't set himself a precise financial goal.

After reflecting briefly, he settled on two hundred and fifty thousand dollars and included it in his formulations, repeating it ad nauseam.

That night, once again seated in front of a rose, he

concentrated and repeated a hundred times, out loud, that he would earn two hundred and fifty thousand dollars from the sale of his screenplay, before three months were over. He took care to include a specific date, avoiding the mistake he'd made with his mentor on the beach.

He had settled on three months instead of two or even one because this time he absolutely wanted to succeed. Later he fell asleep with this astronomical sum dancing before his eyes, imploring his subconscious mind, which he'd nicknamed Sam, to provide him with the inspiration he needed to write a third—and last—draft of his screenplay.

The next morning he awoke in a particularly good mood. And as he got out of bed an idea suddenly popped into his head, perhaps something Sam had planted in his mind while he slept: if he wanted to write a successful screenplay, he should start by studying screenplays that had already proven successful. In fact, this was one of the principles the old man had taught him—that success can be learned by imitating others, by impregnating your mind with the methods and principles used by those who have already attained success.

He remembered the scene in the rose garden, when the old man had explained to him how it was that most millionaires could have guessed why one particular rose had outgrown all the others, although it was of the same variety.

He had to pay more attention to details, to the secret principles that would assure him of the success only a handful of screenwriters and directors achieved.

A sudden idea sparked in his mind, and he chuckled in satisfaction as he acknowledged the source of his inspiration, which he had implored for help the night before—his faithful inner genius, Sam. He decided that he'd rent the hundred most successful movies of the last twenty years and watch them all.

"Defeating the enemy without a fight is the warrior's ultimate achievement," wrote Sun Tzu in the millionaire's testament. Recalling these words of wisdom, John was convinced that his mistake had been to confront the enemy without really being prepared. But by familiarizing himself with the other popular movies, the enemy, he could go about writing his screenplay with a sense of direction. With a definite plan he felt he could accomplish anything.

He was the first customer at the neighborhood video store. He confided his plan to Steve, and through one of those happy coincidences that seem to occur only randomly to those who do not believe in magic, or in the power of their inner wisdom, Steve immediately pulled a copy of *Premiere Magazine* out from under the counter, an issue that just happened to have a list of the last twenty years' top hundred box office hits.

John spent the next two weeks screening seven films a day, until he'd run through the list he'd found "by co-incidence," all except for the celebrated classic *Casablanca*, older than the rest, of course, but in Steve's opinion, and one that John was soon to share, unbeat-able in terms of quality.

Every day Steve would take back the seven movies John had watched and give him seven new ones, some-what astonished by his determination and his desire to learn.

Living like a veritable recluse from morning to night, John ordered pizza, barbecued chicken, and an assort-ment of sandwiches, which he ate while glued to the TV screen. He didn't just watch the movies but, pencil in hand, he took notes and analyzed them.

Whenever he reacted to a scene because it made him laugh or moved him to melancholy, he would ask him-self what had caused his laughter or his tears. He would watch a scene five or ten times until he understood what had happened inside him, which strings the direc-tor had pulled to be able to reach him, to uplift him in some way.

The more movies he watched, the more a pattern began to emerge. He saw principles, constants, charac-

teristics that all great movies had in common. Of
course, he knew you couldn't just follow a set of rules,
you had to be brilliant, original, funny, and above all
moving.

He discovered a series of broad laws of scriptwriting
that he had been completely unaware of before undertaking his study. The millionaire had been absolutely
correct: an observing mind—animated by a specific objective—can see things that minds that are distracted
or lack motivation will overlook. Concentration—this
is where the key to success can generally be found, no
matter what kind of activity you're involved in. His
heart was opening because he had suffered so much the
loss of Rachel. He started thinking with his heart, feeling with his head. He was becoming an artist.

With his study of the hundred movies complete, he
set to work writing the third version of his screenplay.
Literally intoxicated, he felt his concentration improv-
ing from day to day. The heaviness of his paralyzed legs
seemed to give his mind wings, carrying him to heights
of imagination that had hitherto been denied him.

He remembered the millionaire once talking about
the importance of being able to remain physically immobile. "The greatest problem people have," he'd said,
quoting Pascal, "is not to be able to stay in a room by
themselves." John was in the process of discovering the

veracity of those words for himself, as he felt the power that lies hidden in the heart of tranquillity.

He would sometimes spend fifteen or twenty minutes in a state of such deep concentration it almost scared him when he finally snapped out of it. For a few moments, completely absorbed in the task at hand, he'd forget what he was doing, or even who he was. More than once his now constant visitor, the blue jay, startled him out of his reverie, landing on the window ledge to claim its daily allotment of peanuts.

He began to have flashes of inspiration more and more often. His memory became crystal clear, acquiring an almost hallucinatory precision. Tableaux of everything that had occurred over the last few months, as well as scenes from the more distant past, filed through his mind with amazing lucidity.

Such states elated him, filling him with a great sense of joy. He had the impression, the certainty even, that he was discovering a part of himself that up till then had remained unknown, much more luminous, much vaster, and less constricted than the way he'd been used to living and thinking in the past. It was as if all the energy of his being, the energy of his love for Rachel despite their separation and the physical energy his illness prevented him from using, had been transformed, mutated, and was now concentrated in his head: as one door closed, another opened.

At night, after a long day's work that sometimes lasted fifteen hours, he'd often break out into wild fits of laughter, which worried his neighbors. At times he experienced such a deep sense of inner peace and such profound contentment that more than once he thought that if he died right there and then he'd have no regrets.

In two and a half months he'd completely rewritten his screenplay. Then, anxiously, he hurried over to the video store and gave Steve a copy. Steve called back in the middle of the night to tell him that he was overwhelmed, that he hadn't been able to stop reading from beginning to end.

"This is the best script I've read in a year. And that's something, considering that I already knew the story. I'm sure you'll be able to sell it and make a bundle of money. Send it to a few agents and producers right away."

John took Steve's advice and made a dozen copies of the screenplay, which he then sent to the largest Hollywood studios. A month and a half later he received his final letter of refusal. He was devastated. Not only did his failure surprise him—he'd been bursting with confidence when he sent out the scripts—but he'd also done a little personal accounting and realized that his reserves were dangerously low. He could last only a few weeks, a month at most.

Once again he blamed the old millionaire. All the

fine principles he'd revealed weren't worth a damn. He was a charlatan, and John had been tricked. There were no secret laws or principles in this world. It was all just chaos, absurd and violent, and John had been naive enough to believe the contrary.

John went to bed discouraged, but that night he had an astonishing dream. He found himself in his wheelchair at the top of a cliff in the Grand Canyon. A storm sent thunder rumbling through the heavens, and a violent wind whipped huge black clouds together overhead. John tried to turn around so he could get back home, but he found himself incapable of moving his chair even an inch. He grew more and more irritated as the warm rain began falling, soaking his face and clothes.

As he looked behind his chair to see if a stone or a rut was preventing it from moving, he was surprised to see a patch of blue, amazingly clear sky that, in addition to being perfectly circular, also seemed to be moving. In fact, the azure sphere, which shed a column of light on the ground below it, was advancing rapidly in his direction.

John soon realized that the column of light surrounded the old millionaire, who was also in a wheelchair, and who was moving toward him, mysteriously sheltered from the violent storm. The millionaire was soon by his side, smiling calmly and perfectly dry.

"How are you?" he asked.

"Bad," John said.

"I think you need a little shampoo."

And from the pocket of his shabby old overcoat—the same one he'd been wearing in Times Square—he produced a glass bottle containing an extremely brilliant golden liquid, much more brilliant than any ordinary shampoo. In fact, the liquid sparkled as if it were composed of thousands of tiny stars. The old man removed the top and poured the entire contents over John's hair, which he then began massaging vigorously, creating a mountain of foam.

John immediately felt a mysterious energy penetrating his entire being, spreading from the top of his head through the rest of his body and filling him with a sense of calm and joy he had never experienced before. A pleasant sensation of numbness gradually set in, and he felt so good he would have liked to remain sitting there for the rest of his life.

"It's when you think it's all over that things really begin," the millionaire said, massaging John's head energetically. "When you finally renounce your small self, when you realize that all the things it has provided you with to be happy are useless and vain, then your superior self rises like the sun, and you can be touched by celestial grace. You owe me seventeen dollars for the shampoo."

"Seventeen dollars?"

"Just kidding," the millionaire said. He stopped massaging John's head. "You're giving yourself the treatment, not me. But tell me, how is it that you haven't sold your screenplay yet?"

"I don't know."

"Do you *really* believe you can sell it?"

"Yes."

"Are you sure?"

"Yes."

"If you really have faith, you can do anything."

"I really have faith."

"Well, then, prove it to me. If you really have faith, if you can do anything, you can throw yourself over the edge of this cliff with no fear whatsoever."

"Well . . . I mean . . . don't you think you're exaggerating a little here? I . . ."

"Do you have faith or not?"

"Yes."

"Then prove it."

After a moment's hesitation, and despite the folly of the enterprise, John felt that there was no turning back and pushed his chair toward the edge of the cliff, using all his strength to tell himself over and over again that he could make his wheelchair fly like a plane.

And to his complete amazement he actually did fly. The wheelchair plunged into the void, but instead of falling it just floated there, as if it were lighter than air. Astonished and intoxicated by the incredible feeling of being able to fly like a bird, John looked down at the Grand Canyon below him. The storm had subsided, and a magnificent rainbow stretched across the horizon.

Then a doubt assailed him, and his faith faltered. What was happening was impossible. No one could fly without some kind of mechanical support.

Suddenly, like a plane that has lost its engine or had its wings sheared off, he began plummeting toward the ground, shouting desperately for help at the prospect of the certain death awaiting him. Fortunately, he understood in time what had happened: he'd lost his faith, and with it his miraculous power. He immediately began repeating the phrase "I can fly, I can fly" over and over in his mind.

As if by magic he felt himself lifted into the air—he was flying once again. He burst out laughing, elated. A second later the millionaire appeared by his side, like a twin plane, also flying along in his wheelchair.

"You see, it's not that hard. All you need is to really believe. Come on, let's have some fun!"

The old man's wheelchair picked up speed. John

concentrated and managed to catch up to him.

"Don't forget, you can do anything you really believe you can do."

"I won't forget."

"I have to leave you now. I've got some business to take care of."

He accelerated again. John tried to keep up with him but couldn't, and the millionaire soon disappeared, although John did hear his voice, as if amplified by a powerful microphone, filling the sky, repeating what he'd said to John when they'd parted at his Long Island mansion: "You will succeed. Never give up. Never! Never!" And John felt a kind of electric current running though him, galvanizing his being.

The millionaire's voice continued. "Each day is the first day of the rest of your life. Develop the ability to forget about your past failures—or, more precisely, to forget about the disappointment, the melancholy they caused, while retaining the lessons learned from them. Tell yourself that every failure you have encountered is one less failure you'll have to undergo in the future, as long as you've learned the lesson it was meant to teach you.

"So although it may seem paradoxical, every failure actually brings you closer to your goal. Your failures become your power, just another aspect of your future success. They are the price you have to pay. Cultivate in yourself the ability to forget your past frustrations. Clean the slate. Your life begins anew each day. Your determination grows stronger each day, and you approach a success you never dreamed possible. Just persevere.

"Perseverance will overcome all obstacles. Therein lies your true genius. It is the ultimate proof of the veritable love you bring to everything you do. If you really love what you do, if you feel a burning passion for your work, then every experience associated with it will be enriching, and nothing will be a failure.

"Everything you live is meant to teach you something. Failure only exists in the eyes of ordinary persons. There's no shame in making mistakes, in falling. Even Jesus fell three times as he carried the cross. But each time you fall you have to get up again, lifted by the power of your unswerving ideals, even if you hear echoes of mocking laughter and derision all around you, sometimes that of your friends or even your family, those who are supposed to be your partners in life.

"With each failure you encounter your character becomes stronger and your soul more durable. You become more and more the master of your own destiny, because, as the great and profound Heraclitus stated, 'Character equals destiny.'

"Each failure eliminates imperfections of character. The more patiently you can accept failure, the more you evolve, because patience and humility are the virtues of the great. You yourself know that this failure is only a stepping-stone, and when you have climbed all the steps, you will enter the vast plain of success where your harvest will be great, a hundred times greater than you imagined, because you will have given without asking anything in return, and those who give without asking in return can hardly tally their rewards, so great are they.

"Always keep the sublime vision of your objective in mind, the vision of this vast plain where the fruits of wisdom and wealth grow in abundance, and where your soul will soon taste a sublime repose, because it will have made this place its eternal resting place. Prove the nobility of your love, prove the sincerity of your desire and the greatness of faith in your mission. Know that you are eternal. Know that you are greater than failure, and even of success. Never give up. Never. Never . . ."

CHAPTER 21

*In which
the young man risks
everything...*

JOHN AWOKE the next morning filled with new courage. The millionaire's impassioned words resounded in his mind: "You will succeed!" And he remembered his strange dream, in which faith had enabled him to fly through the sky in his wheelchair. Faith! He had to have faith, as strong as steel, that he would sell his screenplay.

He had to persevere. What did a few weeks, a few months, matter, compared to a lifetime? When he succeeded, he'd quickly forget these moments of tribulation. But then he did a rapid calculation of his remaining finances and realized that he could only last for another week or two at most.

Feelings of anxiety pricked at his mind. Had he really done everything he could to sell his screenplay? He started thumbing through the pile of rejection letters he'd received and analyzed each one. As he did so, he realized that some of them were not outright refusals. A number of studios had simply thanked him for submitting his screenplay, explaining that they could not consider accepting "unsolicited" material.

That meant that these studios hadn't even read his screenplay. And it also meant that they couldn't refuse it, since they hadn't acknowledged it in the first place. There was a difference between that and an outright refusal, and so there was still some hope. In any case, that's how John saw it. But how could he get past this barrier of indifference? What strategy could he use?

He had no contacts in the movie business. Of course, he could go knocking on doors, but a man in a wheelchair was not likely to make a very good impression. He began wheeling around his apartment thinking that some physical activity would stimulate his mind and help give him some ideas. However, he couldn't think of anything.

As he rolled past the open door of his clothes cupboard he noticed the ridiculous platform shoes the Cooper Shoe Company had given him as a sample when he'd been working on its publicity campaign.

Without knowing why he leaned over, picked up the

shoes, and looked at them for a while, admiring their excellent craftsmanship and the fine quality of the leather. He repeated to himself that somehow he just had to get his foot in the door of a Hollywood studio, and suddenly a shiver ran down his spine as he had an idea. Get his foot in the door . . . of course! Why not do exactly that!

Half an hour later a truck was at his door, picking up a package he'd addressed to the studio he found most interesting. It was wrapped in bright red paper and tied with red ribbon, and it contained his screenplay, one of the Cooper shoes, and a note that read: "How to get your foot in the door!"

He crossed his fingers and hoped. He prayed, feeling both anxious and elated. He didn't leave his apartment for two days, waiting for a phone call or a letter. But nothing came. After two weeks, when he was on the verge of total despair, the phone finally rang. He hurried to answer. The voice of a woman he didn't know asked if he was John Blake.

"Yes."

"Mr. Ivanovitch would like to talk to you."

He waited with bated breath.

"Mr. Blake?" said a voice charged with energy.

"Yes, that's right."

"I got your little gift a couple of days ago. Clever!

Very clever. And I read your script. I'd like to make you an offer. How about stopping by my office tomorrow?"

"Okay, sure."

"My secretary will arrange the details."

John was transferred back to the secretary, who, after consulting her boss's loaded schedule, finally said she could fit him at three o'clock the following day.

"Uh, tomorrow's a little tight," John said. "I live in New York, as you know, and I've got a lot of things on my agenda these days."

"I would advise you to take the three o'clock appointment for tomorrow," the secretary replied. "My boss is a very busy man. There are hundreds of people out there who would just love to get into his office. He also happens to be leaving Los Angeles for a couple of weeks the day after tomorrow, and by the time he gets back he'll have twenty other hot deals on the table. He might just forget about yours altogether."

"I see. I appreciate your telling me all this, Miss . . ."

"Ford. You're not very familiar with the way things work down here in Hollywood, are you, Mr. Blake?"

"No, not really."

"Well, welcome to the club."

"Thanks. I'll see you tomorrow, then, three o'clock."

"Right. Oh, and one last thing—be on time. Mr. Ivanovitch absolutely hates waiting."

"I will. Thanks."

And he hung up. It was like a dream. He'd succeeded; he was finally going to sell his script. It was
about time! In a few days he would have had to start
looking for a job and forget about his dream of becoming a screenwriter. He had to think fast now. In order to
be in Los Angeles by three o'clock tomorrow he'd have
to catch a flight that very day.

He quickly packed a bag, keeping it light, taking only
the bare essentials. He put on his best suit of clothes,
making sure to wear his father's tie, persuaded that it
would bring him luck. Then he called a taxi and rode
out to the airport, where he presented himself at the
first ticket counter he saw and asked for a flight to L.A.

"There's a plane leaving in half an hour."

"Half an hour! That's perfect. I'll take it."

"All right, that comes to one thousand eight hundred dollars."

"One thousand eight hundred dollars!"

"I only have first-class seats left. I'm sorry."

"What about the next flight?"

"I have another flight at five this afternoon, but it's
full. You . . . well, this is a last-minute booking. If you'd
care to wait I might have a cancellation, but for the moment there's nothing else."

"And tomorrow?"

"Tomorrow, let's see, I have a flight at eleven in the morning, but it's also full. On the other hand, if you can wait until the weekend I have seats available on a number of flights."

"I see. I . . ."

After making a series of rapid and fruitless inquiries at other airline ticket counters—nothing available except a few other first-class seats, even more expensive—John was obliged to return to the first airline he'd tried. He absolutely had to leave that day. He hesitated a moment, gathering courage, and then presented himself at the counter and handed over his Visa card. After all, tomorrow, or in a couple of days at the latest, he'd be a few hundred thousand dollars richer, so why think small and scrimp now?

"I'll take the first-class ticket," he said.

"All right, sir," said the agent, taking his credit card. She calculated the amount plus the tax, and then called for authorization of his card. It was refused.

"I'm sorry, sir. Do you have another card?"

John knew very well that his cards were "maxed out," but he tried the MasterCard anyway. It fared no better than the Visa, and the agent handed it back with an embarrassed look.

"Is there an automatic teller around somewhere?" John asked.

She gave him instructions and watched him roll away in his chair, doubting he'd find a New York–Los Angeles flight that day, and certain that he didn't have enough money for a first-class ticket. Just another dreamer, like so many others in this town . . .

John hurried nervously to the instant banking machine, hoping a few checks he'd written hadn't gone through yet. Lady Luck was with him—he had a balance of $1,914.25 in his account. If he withdrew the money he needed to buy a first-class ticket he'd have only $100 left, which was just about where he'd stood before the old millionaire gave him the $25,000. He was back to square one—even worse, since he might not sell his script and he hadn't paid his rent yet. But there was no turning back now. He punched in a command to withdraw $1,900. The machine responded by saying his daily limit was $500. Damn! He still needed $1,300. He withdrew the $500 anyway, and then entered a command for another $500 withdrawal. The machine announced that he'd reached his daily limit. What to do? He glanced up at one of the large airport clocks. Precious time was ticking by. If he didn't find the rest of the money soon he'd miss his plane, his appointment with the Hollywood producer, and the contract of a lifetime. He rummaged through his things to see if he had his checkbook with him. No. Damn! This was definitely not his day. He rolled away from the automatic teller, heading slowly for the ticket counter, lost in thought. Then he saw something in the window of a money-changing booth that revived his hopes: a Cirrus sticker. His bank card belonged to the Cirrus network. He hurried to the booth, slid his credit card to the clerk, and asked for $1,300.

"American currency?"

"Yes."

"All right, just one moment please." The clerk ran a check on the card, found everything in order, and handed him the money. John was saved. He hurried back to the ticket counter, astonishing the agent by paying for his ticket in cash.

Twenty minutes later he was seated on board the plane, relieved and happy that his audacious maneuver had worked. He was congratulating himself for the umpteenth time when the person sitting next to him arrived.

First-class passengers aren't all very important persons, but all very important persons fly first-class. Because of his infirmity the hostess had placed John in the front row, next to a very important Hollywood agent whose son, paralyzed since birth, was traveling with him.

In his sixties, completely bald, with extremely penetrating eyes that exuded considerable magnetism, Greg

Nicklaus had, for the last twenty years, been a major player on the Hollywood movie scene and now exercised great influence among the major studios, since his clients included some of the most famous actors and directors of the day.

Seeing John in a wheelchair aroused his friendly curiosity. This was enhanced by the fact that John was leafing through his screenplay, making a few last-minute corrections.

"What happened to you?" the agent asked, having seen the hostess help John get out of his wheelchair and into his seat. Because of his son he seemed to be in no way embarrassed to ask such a personal question.

"A spinal thing. My legs are paralyzed."

"Since you were born?"

"No, it's been only a few months."

"My son has never walked," the man said, turning to the charming redheaded boy, about twelve years old, sitting beside him. "The son of my third marriage."

The boy grinned and then plunged back into his comic book.

"Ah, that's too bad. But . . . who knows, maybe he'll be a great genius."

"You think so?" the agent said, sounding surprisingly skeptical. "You're the first person who's ever said that. I mean, it's very kind of you, but I . . ."

And with the candor that people frequently adopt on airplane voyages, due to the fact that the communicants will likely never see each other again, Nicklaus added, "I waited until I was fifty to have a son, and I had John."

"His name's John? So's mine."

"Really! Well, I'm being impolite. I haven't even introduced myself. Greg Nicklaus," he said, extending his hand. "Call me Greg."

"John Blake."

"Are you a writer, John?" the man said, looking down at the screenplay John had closed on his lap.

"Yes, I am. I'm meeting someone called Ivanovitch tomorrow. He's interested in my script."

"Ivanovitch the producer?"

"Yes."

"I know him very well. I'm an agent, by the way," Nicklaus added after a moment. He wasn't used to telling people what he did, since everyone in Hollywood knew who he was.

"Would you like to read my script?" John asked.

"Nobody reads in Hollywood, not even readers. They get their wives or secretaries to read. When a producer tells you he's read a script, he's lying. And if he's not lying, he doesn't work in Hollywood. Just tell me your story in twenty-five words or less."

This was the first time someone had asked John to summarize his screenplay, and he was momentarily at a loss for words.

"If you can't tell me the story in under a minute I won't be able to do it, either, and that's all the time I have. They say that the attention span of people with average intelligence is about twenty minutes. In Hollywood the average attention span is a minute or less."

"I see," John said. He then excused himself, saying he had to go to the washroom.

When he returned to his seat a few minutes later he was astonished as Nicklaus turned to him and said, "You've got a problem with the second act, and your main character is passive for too long before he takes his destiny into his own hands, which annoys the public. Otherwise it's a good script. I cried, I laughed, and I didn't get bored. That's what counts."

The agent could read at phenomenal speed, having mastered the technique of page reading—he could scan a page and absorb its contents in the time it took to turn it—and had evaluated John's script in less than ten minutes.

"You . . . you read the whole thing?" John stammered.

"Yes."

"But I thought nobody reads in Hollywood."

"I don't trust anyone. Some things you can't delegate."

For the rest of the trip the agent, who had really taken a liking to John and found he had talent, told him the story of his life, and then, just before disembarking, handed him his card.

"I'm having dinner with William Goldman, the screenwriter, tomorrow night. Why don't you join us? I'd be happy to see you again. We'll be at the Polo Lounge around eight."

"Sure . . . I . . . I'd like that."

CHAPTER 22

*In which
the young man
discovers the art of
negotiating . . .*

◆

JOHN FOUND a cheap hotel, telling himself that this would probably be the last time he'd have to be so miserly in his choice of accommodations. The evening passed with mixed feelings of elation and sadness—he would so much have liked to share his success with Rachel!

He spent an agitated night and arrived at Ivanovitch's office around two-thirty the next afternoon, making sure to get there early instead of risking being late because of some unexpected delay.

Miss Ford, the secretary, a redhead wearing heavy black eyeglasses, seemed a bit surprised to see him in a wheelchair and, without thinking, said, "If you'd care to sit down and wait . . . I mean . . . if you'd like to wait . . ."

Realizing her tactless blunder, she fell silent, not knowing what to say. John just smiled.

"I'll tell Mr. Ivanovitch you're here."

She picked up the phone, got her boss on the line, and then turned back to John, telling him he'd have to wait a while. Then she took an incoming call, one of many to follow—John was quite amazed at the way the phone kept ringing during the next hour. He listened, fascinated, as he heard all sorts of famous names mentioned, actors, directors, producers, and so on.

Around three-thirty John, who was having trouble hiding his impatience, very politely asked Miss Ford if her boss had forgotten about him.

"I'll remind him," she replied.

After a moment on the phone she said. "He knows you're here. But he's in a meeting with Henry Nichols."

"Henry Nichols . . ." John muttered admiringly. Nichols was one of the most popular stars in Hollywood, so it was perfectly understandable for Ivanovitch not to cut short his discussion just because some unknown scriptwriter by the name of John Blake was waiting to see him.

A half hour later the celebrated movie star strode out of the office, visibly furious. John thought his turn to meet the great producer had finally come.

The secretary called her boss, but he wasn't ready to

see John yet. He was teleconferencing with his lawyers in New York, trying to resolve a legal matter involving his company and a few million dollars.

"He's not ready. He's on the line with New York."

"I see."

"Can you wait a while longer?"

"Sure."

"Don't take it personally. He spends his life putting out fires. Can I get you something in the meantime? Coffee?"

"Okay, thanks."

But even before she could serve him coffee the phone started to ring again. She grew very excited when she found out who was calling—Julia Johnson. At the tender age of twenty-five she was the discovery of the year. Her picture was on the cover of all the magazines, and she already commanded a salary of over five million dollars per picture.

"Oh, Miss Johnson, I . . . Yes, of course. You can't make your seven o'clock appointment with Mr. Ivanovitch? Well, that's no problem. In any case, he's reserved the entire evening for you. Shall we say eight o'clock, then? At the same place? Yes, all right, I've got that down. Same place. Oh, and by the way, I just adored your last picture. You did the right thing at the end, refusing to stay and be his mistress, even if he of-

fered you that beautiful condo and all those credit
cards. He would never have married you. Yes, yes, I understand, I'm sorry, I know how busy you are. I'll give
him the message without fail."

As she was speaking she made a note on a slip of
pink paper, which she threw away after transferring the
information to her computer.

John had to wait another three and a half hours,
each minute becoming more and more interminable.
Shortly after six Miss Ford put down her phone and
said, "Mr. Ivanovitch will see you now."

"At last!" John couldn't help but comment. The secretary opened the office door for him, and then closed it
after he'd rolled into the modern suite, somewhat gaudy
in its display of luxury, and not in the best of taste, at
least in John's opinion.

But what caught his attention most was Ivanovitch's
very unusual appearance—he was so short, just under
five feet two, that he almost disappeared into his black
leather armchair, completely enveloped in a thick
cloud of smoke. The producer, whose tie was almost
wider than his shoulders and whose salt-and-pepper
hair—he was in his fifties—was fashioned into a mili-
tary brush cut, puffed away on an enormous Havana
cigar that he held in his left hand, weighed down by a
heavy Rolex and a few rings that did not exactly suggest

a sense of discretion, although they were worth a small fortune, supporting the claim that good taste does not always come with the first million a person makes.

John had never met anyone quite like him. He exuded incredible energy, but at the same time there was something menacing about him, as if he drew his exceptional magnetism from some secret pact with the devil.

He glued whomever he was facing to the spot with his very blue, very cold, very piercing eyes, and John felt their full impact. They were even more disturbing since Ivanovitch did not even nod in greeting or say a single word, content to examine his visitor as if John were an object of curiosity, some exotic insect. He just stared and kept puffing away on his Havana cigar, blowing a series of perfect smoke rings that he sent floating toward John's embarrassed face.

He finally broke the silence by saying, in his slightly nasal but highly charged, contemptuous voice, "What are you trying to prove?"

The question took John by surprise. Did Ivanovitch think he was playing some kind of game by showing up in a wheelchair? Or was it a display of pity?

"I don't understand."

"Listen, I gave you an appointment for two o'clock this afternoon, and you get here at three. Who do you think you are? You think I have nothing better to do than sit around and wait for you?"

"Your secretary told me the appointment was for three o'clock."

"Are you insinuating that my secretary doesn't know how to do her job?"

"No, not at all. There just happened to be a misunderstanding."

Ivanovitch, whose Armani suit looked a few sizes too big as it hung off his thin, almost emaciated frame, even though his face was full enough and hardly wrinkled—thanks to the best plastic surgeon in Hollywood—got up so swiftly that for a moment John thought he was going to attack him, and he involuntarily recoiled.

"Anyway," Ivanovitch said, moving closer to John in a menacing fashion, "I have some very bad news for you. I had your script read by my top adviser, and he says it's shit. We'd have to pay a whole team of writers to fix it up, and that would cost a fortune."

He reached for a copy of a contract on his desk and literally threw it in John's face.

"All I can offer you is twenty-five thousand, take it or leave it. Sign here and I'll write you a check for twenty-five thousand right now."

He reached into his inside jacket pocket and pulled out a check already made out to John Blake.

"I . . . this is all a little unexpected," said John, looking at the check, which seemed to be accurate—twenty-five thousand dollars, made out to his name.

"Unexpected," Ivanovitch said, inching forward.

"No, it's not that. It's just that . . . this isn't enough. Your check is missing a zero."

"Missing a zero! What are you, crazy? You're telling me my check is missing a zero! You think I'm going to pay two hundred and fifty thousand for the first script written by some illustrious unknown, who, on top of that, rides around in a wheelchair! What are you, nuts? You can pray to God for that amount," he shouted, tearing the check to shreds. John was seized by panic. What would he do without any money? Then, without realizing it, he started repeating a mantra he had learned from the old gardener: "Be at peace and know that I am God." After about a dozen repetitions something strange began to happen.

John was seized by a vision. He saw himself back in the rose garden, standing before the millionaire, who was looking at him with great tenderness. The old man's luminous, profoundly moving gaze, his eyes like two segments of an immense blue sky, filled his entire soul. It was as if time had suddenly stopped, as if all his fears had disappeared.

He just stared right into Ivanovitch's eyes, filled with

a renewed sense of calm. Mysteriously Ivanovitch seemed to be losing his composure, as his expression crumpled into a worried frown. His confidence suddenly evaporated, and he was overcome by a strange kind of fear, something he'd never experienced before.

"You piece of shit, get out of my office! I hope I never see you again, you jerk."

He turned and sat down at his desk, puffing furiously on his cigar. John realized his time was up and hurried out. Once outside the office he stopped for a moment, stunned. It had all happened so quickly, and not at all the way he'd expected.

His heart was racing. Had he just committed a monumental, error? Shouldn't he have accepted the twenty-five thousand dollars? After all, that wasn't bad for a first script. But an inner voice had told him to hold back at the last moment.

He wanted more. He'd set himself a goal: two hundred and fifty thousand dollars. But maybe that was a mistake. Maybe he'd aimed too high and passed up an opportunity that probably wouldn't come around again for a very long time. Had he missed a unique chance to get his foot in the Hollywood door? Had he been too greedy?

How naive he'd been to think that the sale of his script was nothing more than a formality. And yet why had Ivanovitch, who'd been so polite and enthusiastic on the phone, suddenly changed his attitude so unexpectedly?

If John had known more about the ins and outs of Hollywood wheeling and dealing, he'd have realized that Ivanovitch's behavior was simply a common negotiation tactic, used to unsettle, and at times completely humiliate, an opponent. In fact, negotiating was Ivanovitch's favorite pastime, and this particular strategy of intimidation had allowed him to sign a number of incredibly lucrative deals with beginners, and even with experienced artists whose flagging careers and temporary financial difficulties made them vulnerable to this kind of pressure.

CHAPTER 23

*In which
the young man
outfoxes the fox . . .*

JOHN TOOK a few deep breaths to calm down, telling himself to listen to his inner voice, which always operated with good reason. But what could that reason be? He had to find out fast, very fast indeed. Hadn't the old gardener told him that everything always works out for the best and that it is only because of the restrictions of our own mind that we are not able to see the advantages, the deep and mysterious reasons for all events, even those that appear to be obstacles and causes of misfortune?

Curiously, perhaps because his situation was so desperate, and because his prayer had been absolutely sincere—or simply because necessity is the mother of invention—a solid plan came to mind.

He went up to Miss Ford, the secretary, who was at her desk, surprised to see him so soon.

"Finished already?" she asked.

"Yes. Things didn't work out exactly as I would have liked."

"That's too bad."

"But I wanted to ask you a little favor. I'd like to know where Mr. Ivanovitch is meeting Julia Johnson tonight."

"I'd really like to help you, but that information is strictly confidential."

"You'd be doing me a great favor."

"I know, but I really can't."

"Well, can you tell me if they're supposed to meet in a public place? I mean, a place anyone could go, just out of coincidence. Your boss would never know who told me."

Miss Ford hesitated, but before she could reply her phone rang again and she took the call. John glanced over and by a stroke of luck noticed the pink slip of paper on which Miss Ford had noted the change in arrangements for her boss's meeting with Julia Johnson. Unfortunately, all he could make out was the name "Julia Johnson" and not the location of their rendezvous. He was about to lean over and retrieve the paper when Miss Ford hung up and turned back to him.

"So, how about it?" John said.

"I can't do it," she replied. "If my boss ever found out I'd lose my job. The rules about confidentiality are very strict around here. We deal with so many famous—"

The phone rang again and John took advantage of the distraction when Miss Ford swiveled around in her chair to look for a document in the filing cabinet behind her desk. This was his chance. Leaning over, he saw it. There was Julia Johnson's name across the top, and below it the time and above all the place of her meeting with Ivanovitch: the Polo Lounge!

It seemed the gods were with him, since he was supposed to be at the Polo Lounge himself that evening to join the powerful agent he'd met on the plane. The coincidence made his plan a lot easier to carry out.

He hurried out of the building and rolled to a stop in front of the first phone booth he found. He took the agent's card out of his pocket and dialed the number, saying, "He has to be there! He has to be there" over and over to himself. Luckily, Greg Nicklaus, being a confirmed workaholic, was still in his office.

"Mr. Nicklaus? John Blake here. We were supposed to get together tonight at the Polo Lounge."

"Is there a problem?"

"No, no, I just wanted to ask you a little favor. I met Mr. Ivanovitch, the producer, and I was a little disappointed by his offer, only a hundred and fifty thousand for my screenplay. I know I can do a lot better. In fact, I have solid information that assures me I can. His secretary told me he already has a buyer interested, one of the major studios, but she wouldn't tell me which one."

"And you want me to find out for you."

"No, it's much easier than that. I'm supposed to see him at the Polo Lounge this evening, before my meeting with you. All I'd like you to do is come over and say hello. When he sees that I know an agent as influential as you are he'll get nervous and offer me what I want."

Nicklaus burst out laughing.

"That sounds like a smart idea to me to jack up the value of your material in three simple steps."

"That's about it."

"No problem. I'll see you this evening, and I'll come by your table and make the big play."

"Thanks," said John, "I really appreciate it." He hung up, elated. The first part of his plan looked like it would work out, as long as everything kept going according to schedule and nothing unexpected occurred.

At five minutes to eight John made his entrance at the Polo Lounge, an entrance that did not go unnoticed, as it was highly unusual to see someone in a wheelchair at the watering hole patronized by some of the biggest players in Hollywood.

"Do you have a reservation, sir?" the maître d' asked with some skepticism, since John's was not a familiar face, nor was he dressed in the fashion he was used to seeing on most of his regular customers.

"Yes, I'm meeting Mr. Nicklaus. Greg Nicklaus."

Greg Nicklaus happened to be one of the most frequent and important of the Polo Lounge's clients, and the management always kept one of its best tables reserved for him. The face of the maître d' lit up in a broad smile as he realized he'd narrowly avoided committing a major blunder.

"If you'd care to follow me, sir, Mr. Nicklaus and his guest have already arrived."

John followed, and he soon saw the agent and his guest seated at the far end of the room. Then he noticed Ivanovitch, excused himself, and told the maître d' he'd join Mr. Nicklaus in a moment, he just wanted to have a few words with the producer first.

"No problem," the maître d' said, leaving John to make his way to Ivanovitch's table, where the producer sat chatting over cocktails with the celebrated actress Julia Johnson, causing a number of heads to turn.

Seeing John approach, Ivanovitch went purple with rage. What was this little idiot doing here? Why was he coming to his table? He was about to tell him to get lost when John, with an assurance that surprised even himself, extended his hand to Julia Johnson and introduced himself.

"It's a pleasure to meet you, Miss Johnson. My name is John Blake. My agent, Greg Nicklaus, told me you liked my script a lot, and said he hopes you'll decide to do the female lead. I can only say that I'd be flattered if you take the part. I consider you to be one of the greatest artists of our time."

Julia Johnson offered her hand in return, and John, with somewhat outmoded gallantry, kissed it.

"No one reads in Hollywood," Greg Nicklaus had told him. So it was that all the "players" were obliged to lie instead of admitting they hadn't read something and possibly passing up a golden opportunity. Julia Johnson was no exception to the rule, which is why she declared, "You're absolutely right. I adored your script."

Ivanovitch was beginning to think he'd made a terrible mistake in letting John's script get away from him. With Julia Johnson's signature on a contract, financing even the most ambitious of projects became a piece of cake. Why hadn't this bastard Blake mentioned that she was interested in the first place? Or that his agent was the all-powerful Greg Nicklaus? Maybe it was all just a bluff. . . .

But his growing suspicions were quickly dissolved as Greg Nicklaus himself, right on schedule, walked over to say hello to John. However, out of politeness, as well as a sense of respect for the Hollywood pecking order, he greeted Julia Johnson first.

"Julia, always a great pleasure. We should do lunch one day soon."

"Yes, I'd like that. We can use the occasion to talk some more about John's script."

"If John has no objection," Nicklaus joked.

Ivanovitch found all this friendly banter highly disconcerting. Something big was going on that he didn't know about, and being left out in the cold was one of the things he feared most in the world.

"Igor, how's it going?" Nicklaus said.

"I never felt better in my life," Ivanovitch replied through clenched teeth.

"Well, I have to be going," Nicklaus said. Turning to John, he added, "Don't be too long here, John. We're about to order."

"I'll just be a few minutes."

While Julia took a call on her miniature cellular phone, Ivanovitch watched the agent walk off and paled with rage. Julia seemed to be involved in an animated discussion, and Ivanovitch took advantage of the occasion to pull John aside for a little private conversation.

"Listen, I wasn't aware of all the factors involved in

this deal, but after you left my office I had one of my best directors read your script."

Lowering his voice, he continued, "I'm ready to add that zero to your check. I'm offering you the two hundred and fifty grand you wanted. But I need an answer right away."

"Listen," John said, "give me twenty-four hours to think it over."

"Three hundred and fifty thousand," Ivanovitch hissed, raising the stakes considerably.

"I'll get back to you tomorrow, without fail," John said, courageously holding his ground. He waved good-bye to the actress, who acknowledged the gesture distractedly. Ivanovitch watched, fists and teeth clenched, as John carefully made his way between tables. He'd close this deal if it was the last thing he did.

John joined the agent and his guest, both of whom were waiting impatiently.

"I'm so happy to meet you, Mr. Goldman," John said, extending his hand. "I've read all your screenplays, and I think they're fabulous."

"This isn't Mr. Goldman," the agent corrected him. "This is Mr. Zeller, producer at large."

"Oh, well," said John, blushing at his mistake.

"There's been a little change of program," Nicklaus explained. "When you called me at my office I was in a meeting with Lazarus—Mr. Zeller, I mean. He's usually interested in the same type of project Ivanovitch tends to go for. In fact, Ivanovitch used to work for Mr. Zeller, and if he doesn't mind . . ." He turned to Zeller for permission to go on, and the producer nodded his head. "I may say that our old friend Igor managed to get away with stealing quite a few of Mr. Zeller's projects."

"While we're on the subject," John said, "I want to thank you for the little favor you did me. It worked like a charm. Ivanovitch offered me three hundred and fifty thousand."

"You're welcome," the agent said. "Oh, and incidentally, Julia Johnson really *is* interested in the lead role."

Zeller, who had adopted a Mediterranean style of dressing and was always seen wearing a large Panama hat and very light colored suits, pursed his lips when he heard the amount Ivanovitch was offering, but at the mention of Julia Johnson's name his eyes lit up with particular intensity. He entered into the conversation by saying, "Listen, kid, I don't feel like getting into a price war with one of my ex-employees. I'm interested in your script, but I'm not the type to play games. I'm ready to offer you half a million, right now. But not a penny more. And that doesn't include dinner."

"Half a million!"

John glanced at the agent for help. Nicklaus nodded

his head, indicating that he should jump at the deal.

"I . . . I really don't like to accept an offer without thinking it over."

The producer pulled out his checkbook and a large fountain pen.

"Do I sign this damn check or not?" he demanded.

"Well . . . okay, you talked me into it."

The producer signed the check, but before handing it over he took two copies of a contract out of an envelope and filled in the amount of the transaction on each. He had John sign them and then gave him the check. John, out of habit—and also because he'd never seen a check as large as this one before—quickly verified the amount.

"Four hundred thousand?" he said, surprised. "I thought you said five hundred thousand."

"By signing the contract," Nicklaus explained, "you agreed to take me on as your agent. I get a twenty percent commission."

"A hundred thousand dollars? For an hour's work?" John protested.

"I know, it's depressing. I used to earn a lot more when I was younger. I'm losing my touch."

John wasn't sure if he was joking or serious, but he didn't press the point. After all, the agent had a right to his cut, since the little favor he'd done for John had paid off beyond his wildest expectations, and John hadn't been completely honest either when he'd told Nicklaus that Ivanovitch had made an offer of a hundred and fifty thousand dollars, simply in order to get some other producer interested or to get Nicklaus to become his agent.

The fact that Greg Nicklaus was making some money did a lot to alleviate his conscience for using the more or less dishonest means he had resorted to. But hadn't it been Nicklaus himself who had taught John that one of the first things he should know about Hollywood was that no one ever read anything and, second, that everyone lied?

Chapter 24

*In which
the young man
discovers the reason
for his
tribulations . . .*

◇

THE FIRST thing John did when he got back to New York was to hurry to his bank in order to deposit the check.

When he'd concluded his business at the bank, John decided to pay a visit to his mentor, the person who had played such a crucial role in his success, even if things hadn't worked out exactly as he'd predicted.

Henry, the butler, answered the door. He greeted John with a surprised smile and said, "What happened to you, sir?" in reference to John's wheelchair.

"Oh, it's a spinal thing. Even my doctor can't say for sure what it is. Is he here?"

"Yes, he's out in the garden. Shall I accompany you, sir?"

"Thanks, I know the way."

At the entrance to the rose garden John found a magnificent white rose lying on the gravel of one of the pathways. He bent over to pick it up. It was a Polar White variety, and John had not seen as exquisite a blossom in the entire rose garden. As he moved forward he discovered where it came from—a bush growing near the spot where the sickly rosebush had stood, one he'd never noticed before.

John had thought that the sick bush had died, and he was astonished to find that this was not the case. Instead, it was flourishing, covered with astoundingly beautiful white blossoms. In fact, it was this same bush that had produced the exquisite specimen he held in his hand.

So the millionaire had finally managed to bring it back to health! John remembered what the old man had said about it: "Every time I see this rosebush, I think of you. The only reason I came back was to take care of it."

John felt greatly moved, since he, too, had experienced a mysterious and beautiful spiritual healing. Filled with emotion, he pushed the wheels of his chair as quickly as he could down the path.

He found the old man in the center of the rose garden, bent over a bush he was pruning with great care, dressed in clothes John had never seen him wear before: a long white tunic and a pair of black sandals.

Despite its simplicity, the outfit gave him a very noble, majestic air, the tunic being gathered at the waist
by a modest piece of rope. Instead of calling out a greeting, John held back and decided he'd play a little joke
on his old friend.

The last time they'd met John had been frustrated in
his efforts to set the mysterious metal sphere spinning
solely through the power of concentration. But he felt
that since then he'd made considerable progress in mas-
tering the power of his mind. He felt like trying his luck
once again. He concentrated on the sphere with all his
might. Nothing happened the first few seconds, and
then, suddenly, the sphere moved.

John felt a shiver run up his spine. Had he improved
as much as that? Could he use his mental power to
make the sphere turn as easily as the millionaire? Unless it was the wind. But then the sphere slowed down,
and in a few seconds stopped altogether, leaving John
perplexed as to whether or not his newfound ability to
make objects move from a distance was real. He tried
again, realizing that his sudden joy and sense of pride
had distracted him so that he'd stopped concentrating.

After a few seconds the sphere began spinning once
more, even faster this time, until it emitted its unique
and mysterious sound.

The millionaire looked up, intrigued, studying the treetops to see if the wind had picked up. But there was only a very gentle breeze, quite insufficient to set the sphere spinning so fast. The young man stopped concentrating, the sphere slowed to a halt, and the millionaire bent over and resumed his horticultural labors.

John began again, this time concentrating with as much intensity as he could muster. In obedience to his will the sphere started turning, rapidly picking up speed until its strange music sounded once more, attracting a flock of birds, as it had on the previous occasion. The ducks in the pond were also affected and soon formed a perfect circle around the sphere's base.

Some birds even alighted on John's shoulders, which surprised him greatly. What special charm had he developed while living the life of a recluse, to be able not only to set the sphere spinning but also to attract birds to his person, just like Saint Francis of Assisi? Was the power of concentration so great, so mysterious?

The millionaire interrupted his work once again, distracted by the music of the sphere. He soon realized that it wasn't the wind that was responsible and looked around until he finally spotted John.

"So, you've arrived at last," he said with a broad smile, as if John's presence didn't surprise him in the least, as if he'd known he was coming.

"Yes," said John, at the same time relaxing his effort to concentrate, so that the sphere slowed down and the birds dispersed.

"I see you've made quite a lot of progress," the millionaire said, turning to look at the sphere, which had almost stopped spinning.

"Yes, I have," John replied. "But the secret you revealed to me for achieving success didn't work. I set myself a goal of two hundred and fifty thousand . . ."

"And?"

"And I made four hundred thousand."

"Well, nobody's perfect," the old man said with a chuckle.

"Yes, I'd agree with that," John said, indicating his wheelchair. "I really would have liked you to be there when the going got really tough."

"I was there, all the time, by your side. I sometimes even had to carry you on my shoulders, when your strength gave out. But your eyes weren't open, and you didn't see me."

The reply moved John greatly. But what the millionaire said next surprised and intrigued him even more.

"In fact, I helped you more than you know. Because if you hadn't spent these last few months in a wheelchair, it would have taken you years to achieve success. And the reason you're in a wheelchair is because of the wine I gave you to drink the last time we met."

"You mean I'm handicapped . . . or sick, at least . . . because of you?" John demanded with mounting anger. He gripped the wheels of his chair, as if he had to hold back from physically attacking the old man.

"You told me you were ready to pay any price for attaining your objectives. I distinctly recall asking you a number of times."

"Had I known that being sick was the price I'd have to pay, I'd never have accepted. Now I have to spend the rest of my life handicapped."

"The legs of your body had to die, at least for a while, so that those of your mind could start living. You see, now you can turn the sphere, where before you couldn't. So I helped you attain your goal. Why, then, are you angry?"

"I don't want to spend the rest of my life in this wheelchair! The doctors all say there's no hope."

"What do doctors have to do with it? What they say doesn't matter—it's your mind that counts. Only your mind. Have you already forgotten what I told you? That faith can move mountains? If you believe you can get out of that wheelchair and walk, if you really believe it, then you can do it. And no one in the whole world can stop you."

"Don't think I haven't tried, dozens of times, hundreds of times," John cried. And he tried standing up, using all his strength, all his concentration, but in vain. His forehead damp with sweat, his face blue from the effort, he finally slumped back into the chair, head bowed, his lips distended in a despairing grin.

"You see?" John hissed.

"No, I don't see. You remind me of certain people who are so convinced that they cannot succeed they do everything they can to fail, and then go around bragging that they were right because they failed!"

"Success is one thing, being handicapped is another."

"Why do you keep sitting there in that wheelchair?" the millionaire demanded, his voice suddenly booming with energy and power, as if he, too, were angry, or on the verge of becoming so.

"Because my legs are paralyzed!"

"Who is paralyzed?" the millionaire countered with his curious logic, demonstrating, as usual, his singularly maieutic approach to solving problems.

"I am, for God's sake! Don't you recognize me?"

"What is this 'you'?"

"Me . . . I am me!" John shouted, exasperated, not having a clue what the old man meant.

"You're not in a wheelchair. Not your real self. You are all mind. You are not a body. A body is only an illusion. Your real self is immortal and all-powerful. And so

I say, if you have faith, if you understand what I just said, then get up and walk."

John felt a series of strange shivers run through his body. The millionaire's words were not a simple command, they were like powerful waves of energy entering into him, galvanizing him, making his entire body tremble. It was a feeling he'd never experienced before.

He pushed down with all his strength on the chair's armrests and stretched out his legs. With great effort he managed to reach a standing position, but then his faith faltered, and after a few seconds he fell back into his wheelchair. Head bowed once again, ashamed, with tears streaking down his face, he was convinced that he was condemned to be infirm for the rest of his life.

It was then that the millionaire seemed to enter a strange state. He lifted his eyes heavenward, as if imploring some superior power, raised his right arm as well, and began murmuring a mysterious sound, softly at first, and then more and more loudly.

It was a very ancient mantra, "Iu," which he chanted only on rare occasions and which possessed amazing qualities. He pronounced the "I" like the vowel "e," which he stretched out for at least five seconds, and which he modulated in a nasal, strangely metallic voice. This was followed by the vowel "u," which he pronounced like the "ou" in *you*.

The wind picked up and clouds began gathering overhead, as if a storm were approaching. The metallic sphere began spinning, emitting its music, and birds flocked around, not only flying in circles around the sphere but over the millionaire's head as well. They would sometimes swoop up in a great arc toward the sky, as if following the trajectory his index finger was indicating. Then they would plunge back toward him, all packed together into a strange and fascinating ball of flight. Soon lightning rent the sky and thunder rumbled from afar.

John had no idea what was going on, nor did he know how to react. He was quite simply terrified. But he soon grew even more frightened as Horace, the lion, erupted through a hedge into the center of the rose garden, snarling in rage. When he saw John, the lion stopped in its tracks, stood stock-still for a moment, and then charged, as if attacking some helpless prey, the docile pet suddenly transformed into a wild beast that would give no quarter and show no pity.

For an instant John stopped functioning with his mind and became pure instinct, entering a state of pure "zen," so to speak, without his being aware of it. He forgot that he'd been paralyzed for months, leaped out of his chair, and ran for his life. Where faith had failed, fear succeeded. He didn't have to run for long, as the millionaire lowered his arms and ceased his mysterious chanting to call to Horace, who immediately trotted up to him and rolled over at his feet.

The wind dropped all at once, leaving the clouds overhead immobilized; the flocks of birds returned to their roosts; and the sphere stopped spinning.

John turned around and saw that the lion wasn't chasing him anymore but was, instead, rolling around like a pussycat under its master's caress. And it was only then that he realized he was standing up and walking. All trace of his illness had disappeared. He couldn't believe it. He was cured! What had happened? Another miracle? Would he ever understand the mysterious power his mentor seemed to possess?

He walked toward the millionaire, keeping an eye on the lion to make sure its hunting instinct didn't reawaken.

"What happened?" he asked, his eyes filled with tears of gratitude.

"Your illness was no longer necessary. It was given to you as a kind of grace, to help develop your mind more rapidly. Otherwise it would have taken years, maybe even lifetimes, to get to the same point. I told you, the soul does not measure time in the same way most people do. Since it was no longer necessary, your paralysis disappeared. The same goes for all suffering and all calamities—they are sent to us out of mercy to help us evolve and find our true selves, find the real force within us, which ordinary happiness prevents us from seeing, because it lulls us to sleep—or, rather, allows us to remain asleep. . . .

"People who are tested are fortunate. But when you find your true self, suffering is no longer necessary. And not only is it no longer necessary, it is no longer possible. There is only room for happiness, for renewed rejoicing. . . ."

The millionaire leaned down and stroked Horace affectionately, then made a sign with his hand, instructing the great cat to leave them.

The young man started crying, overcome by an extraordinary emotion, a boundless sense of gratitude more intense than anything he'd ever felt before. Filled with immense love, he walked over to the old man and took a place at his feet. As he kneeled and touched his white robe, he felt a great sense of peace. The millionaire ran a hand through John's hair, caressing him.

The two men remained still for a solemn moment, filling the space around them with peace and inexpressible love. Then the millionaire broke the magical silence by saying, "Stand up. I have to leave now."

"Already?" John asked, getting to his feet, almost panic-stricken, much to his own surprise, as if the millionaire had just told him some terrible news.

The millionaire waited a few seconds before answering, gazing at John with great affection, like a father at his son.

"What I had to do here is accomplished. We should not dally once our work is done. I'm leaving to rejoin my brothers."

"But . . ." the young man stammered, struck by a sudden sadness that brought tears to his eyes. "Will we see each other again one day?"

"Who knows?" the millionaire replied.

"Can't I come with you? Leave with you?"

"No, you aren't ready. There are still things you have to achieve here. We should never leave before taking care of everything first; otherwise we have to come back," the old man explained.

"But . . . I don't have anything left to do."

"Do you really think so? Aren't there some things you haven't settled yet? With a certain woman, for example?"

Of course, John immediately thought of Rachel, although he'd never mentioned her to the old millionaire. How did he know about her, then? Another mystery he wouldn't have time to figure out, since at that moment Edgar, the chauffeur, arrived with a large box wrapped in bright red paper and tied with a gold ribbon.

"The limousine is ready, sir," Edgar said, bowing first to the millionaire and then to John.

"Ah, Edgar, I see you brought the gift. That's good." Turning to John, he said, "I'm offering you this, but only on one condition."

"What?"

"That you don't open it out of simple curiosity, or because I'm offering to you, but only when you feel you really need to."

"Of course."

"And I hope you don't throw it in the river like the last gift I gave you."

John turned crimson. How had his mentor been able to guess what he'd done all those months ago, throwing the old box into the East River in a gesture of despair?

But there was no time to ask questions as the millionaire nodded to Edgar and the chauffeur handed over the gift. His first reflex was to begin unwrapping it, but then he remembered the promise he'd just made and, ashamed, patted it admiringly, discreetly replacing the bow he'd begun to untie.

The old man returned his smile.

"I . . . I don't know if one day I'll be able to express my gratitude for all you've taught me. I . . . How can I ever thank you enough? I know I don't have much compared to you, but ask me for something . . . anything . . ."

"Anything?" the millionaire said.

"Yes," he said shyly.

"Well, then, I'd like your tie."

"My tie?" the young man said, reaching up to touch it, a protective reflex. "I . . . I don't see what you could . . ."

"You said I could ask you for anything."

"Yes, but this tie is very special for me."

"Why do you think I'm asking for it?"

"It's . . . it's the tie my father was wearing when he died. It has great sentimental value. . . . I could buy you one just like it. . . . Ask me for anything," said the young man desperately, "but not for this."

"I understand," the millionaire said. "It was too much. It's time we went our ways now."

"I . . . no, wait . . . I . . ."

With tears in his eyes John undid the knot of his father's tie, a knot he had never opened since his father's death. He took the tie off and handed it to the millionaire, who accepted it with a benevolent smile.

The instant John let go of the tie, he felt a great calm, a new sense of lightness, within his being. It was as if all the pain, all the sadness connected to his father's death had suddenly, magically evaporated. He felt free—liberated, to be more precise—relieved of an invisible burden that had weighed heavily on him for months.

The millionaire seemed to understand what was happening, and his smile broadened as he knotted the tie around his neck. With his white tunic and sandals it made for a rather bizarre outfit!

"How do I look?" he asked John when he'd finished knotting the tie.

John could hardly contain his mirth and, unable to control himself any longer, burst out laughing. The millionaire joined in, as did Edgar—after some hesitation and despite the reserve he habitually exercised whenever his patron was present. They laughed until their sides hurt, and when the millionaire calmed down at last he said, "I guess I should wear this tie often, since it really seems to have an effect on people. Now, John," he said, pausing, "it's really time for you to leave."

"Now?"

"Yes. You don't have a minute to lose. You have to see this woman very soon. The stars are aligned in a way that won't occur again for a very long time. If you don't see her in the next few hours, you'll lose her for nine more years. Go. And don't pay too much attention to appearances. Listen only to your heart."

Greatly moved, John put the gift on the ground and threw himself into his mentor's arms, holding him close for a long moment. How could he ever express his gratitude? he wondered. But there was no time to ask questions as the millionaire pushed him away, saying simply, "Go now. You don't have much time."

And so John took his leave of the old millionaire, his heart heavy and at the same time anxious at the thought of seeing Rachel, whom he'd believed was the woman of his life and who was now involved with another man. What would he say to her?

The truth, the simple truth. She at least had a right to know what had really happened, that he hadn't left her because he didn't love her but because he hadn't wanted to burden her with a paralyzed husband. He couldn't help thinking that, despite his professional success, life was not perfect, far from it.

He was not paralyzed any longer, and he was rich, or in any case sheltered from need for a good many years to come. But Rachel was not free.

However, he had more or less promised the millionaire he'd see her. He'd seemed to think it was of the utmost importance. So he'd have to take the chance, even at the risk of a broken heart.

CHAPTER 25

*In which
the young man
discovers the
nobility of love . . .*

IN HER apartment, which she'd insisted on keeping until the very last moment, Rachel was almost finished with the preparations for her wedding. She wore a beautiful white dress, designed especially for her condition—she was more than eight months pregnant. Louis Renault, her fiancé, had insisted the wedding take place before the birth.

Standing in front of her mirror, and at the same time keeping a watchful eye on the two children in her apartment—Jennifer was to be her flower girl and Jose, her best man—Rachel adjusted her veil.

For a woman who was going to get married in just a few hours she didn't seem to be bursting with joy. Instead, she seemed somewhat melancholy. Was it the fatigue caused by a first pregnancy? Or was it the music playing on her sound system, the strains of "Unforgettable" that brought back memories she'd tried so hard to banish from her mind?

The children, very excited, kept running in and out of the apartment and up and down the hallway, despite Rachel's repeated, albeit unconvincing, warnings to be more quiet. So when John arrived he didn't get a chance to ring the bell or even knock on the door, which was already wide open. He walked in and found Rachel standing in front of her mirror. Rachel looked stunning, John thought with a pang of jealousy, but looking closer, he was shocked. She was pregnant.

He immediately wondered what he was doing there, why the old millionaire had pressed him to come and see her. The best thing would be to just turn around and leave without saying a word to her. After all, what was there to say? Tell her the truth? Yes, he would have at least liked to tell her the truth, the reason he'd decided to break up with her. But was such a revelation appropriate on her wedding day? Wouldn't it be terribly selfish of him to talk about all that now?

He was also surprised to hear "Unforgettable" playing on the sound system. Was it just a coincidence, or was it a sign that she was nostalgic and still thought about their love? He didn't get a chance to listen to Nat

King Cole's crooning for very long, as Rachel turned around to bring the children to order and saw him standing there, whereupon the first thing she did was to hurry over and turn off the music.

They stood looking at each other for a moment, silent, lost in their emotions. John had never in his life thought he'd have to deal with a situation as painful as this. The woman who, despite everything, he still considered to be his lifelong mate was pregnant by, and about to marry, another man. The woman he'd lost because he hadn't wanted to burden her. And the worst of it, the most ironic part of it all, was that now he was in perfect health, and rich to boot!

It seemed to him that everything had its price. If he hadn't suffered so much after leaving her, he wouldn't have discovered the inner sensitivity that led him to write a moving screenplay. His suffering had opened his heart and given birth to his talent. . . .

But in exchange he'd lost the woman he loved. Was this what the millionaire wanted him to learn when he'd insisted he find Rachel before it was too late? Why this renewed torture, this humiliation, this heartache at having to watch her leave him forever for another man?

"John?" Rachel couldn't help but say when she saw him. "Children, go wait out in the hallway, would you?" Rachel said.

Despite their tender age, the children seemed to understand the seriousness of the situation and docilely filed outside.

Rachel fell silent. She didn't know what to say. Of course, she would have liked to tell him she'd been madly in love with him, and perhaps loved him still. But he'd left her.

She'd felt abandoned, and justifiably so. And in her desperation she'd warmed to the unswerving friendship offered her by Louis Renault. He had consoled her during her months of sorrow and was now ready to offer her everything, even to the point of forgetting that he was her second choice.

Louis had never taken advantage of the situation but had always been noble and magnanimous in his admiration. She couldn't say as much for John, who had first seduced her and then abandoned her.

These thoughts hardened her heart, and the emotions she felt on seeing him again after so long dissipated. She waited, on the defensive again.

"I . . . I didn't know that you . . ." John began.

He didn't dare utter the fatal words, those painful words, the words that were tearing him apart: that she was getting married, yes, she was getting married, and that she was pregnant.

"Yes, in about an hour" was all she said. She brought

a hand up to her stomach, as if in pain.

"I . . . I . . ." John stammered. "I just wanted to see you one last time, to tell you . . . to tell you that I left you not because . . . because I stopped loving you. I was sick, I thought it was incurable . . . I was paralyzed . . . and I didn't want to burden you with a handicapped husband."

For an instant she doubted him. Was he telling the truth? She looked straight into his eyes and saw that he wasn't lying, that he was deeply distressed and suffering terribly.

A handicapped husband! So he had wanted to marry her! He hadn't left just to get rid of her. At last she comprehended the scope of the terrible misunderstanding that had separated them.

His motive had been noble and pure. She felt dizzy, and her eyes grew moist. But he was too late. Life had decided on another destiny for them. Fate can be cruel, Rachel thought.

How beautiful she looked in her wedding dress! John thought. More beautiful than she'd ever been, with her shining chestnut hair softened by her filmy veil. Her eyes had never been so green, so bright. Saddened, John decided it would be best if he left.

"Well, I . . . I should be going. I . . . I wish you all the happiness in the world."

She wanted to tell him she still loved him, that not a day went by without her thinking about him. But she couldn't; Louis had been too kind. She had to be strong and resist the temptation.

For his part, John felt like taking her in his arms and kissing her one last time, persuaded as he was that he'd never see her again. But he just wasn't able to. Her wedding gown, her pregnancy . . . so many problems, so many obstacles in the way . . .

As he turned to leave, he was surprised to see Louis Renault enter the apartment, accompanied by Gloria, his ex-fiancée. Despite her disappointment at seeing him marry another woman, her friendship for him had been stronger than her jealousy, and since she was his best friend, she had agreed to serve as a witness.

Louis Renault was no less surprised to see John on his wedding day, of all days. What was he doing here? As far as he knew, John hadn't been invited.

Needless to say, both John and the future bride-groom felt extremely ill at ease. Gloria had no idea who John was, nor did she know anything about his relationship with Rachel. Louis, a proud fellow to say the least, had not made a point of publicizing Rachel's unhappy past.

Looking very elegant in a light dress and a huge white hat, Gloria smiled at John, thinking he was another guest until she noticed the somber suit he was wearing, not at all appropriate for a wedding.

But there was no time for conversation or even for introductions as Rachel, affected by the shock of seeing John after so long, was suddenly overcome with dizziness and, clutching her belly, had to be helped into a chair. She cried out in pain—her contractions had begun.

"It's coming," she said in alarm. "I can feel it coming. I have to get to the hospital."

Louis Renault hurried to her side, helped her to her feet, and supported her down the stairs. The children, waiting outside, soon realized what was happening.

"I guess the marriage is off for today," said one.

"Looks like it," said the other.

Fortunately for them, Louis Renault, showing remarkable presence of mind and common sense, threw them a twenty-dollar bill, suggesting they go and eat some pizza as a consolation prize. Since the celebrated lawyer, it will be remembered, drove a two-seater sports car, there was no room for Gloria.

"Can I get a ride with you?" she asked John.

He hadn't thought he'd have to bear the pain of watching the woman he loved so deeply get married to another man, never mind watching her give birth to his child. But under the circumstances, how could he refuse? He held the door open as Gloria climbed into his Mustang. The millionaire's present, still in its red wrapping, was on the back seat. Gloria thought it was a wedding gift.

John trailed the sports car as it sped toward the hospital, running a few red lights when there was no danger.

"Are you a member of the family?" Gloria asked John.

"A friend," he said, still stunned by what had taken place. He wondered if the old millionaire had known what he'd have to face by going to see Rachel.

In the car ahead, Rachel was making a great effort not to deliver the baby. "It wants to come out!" she cried. "It wants to come out. Hurry, Louis, hurry up!"

"We're almost there, just hold on," Louis said, trying to calm her down.

Rachel still didn't know if she was going to have a boy or a girl. She'd had a couple of ultrasound tests done during the course of her pregnancy, but, like a good novelist, she'd preferred to keep the suspense going until the very end.

They got to the hospital about twenty minutes later.

The staff on duty in the obstetrics ward found it a little strange when they were confronted with a woman in a wedding gown about to give birth, and there was some confusion at first. But the urgency of the situation precluded asking too many questions—there wasn't even enough time to take off her wedding dress.

In the commotion that followed, Gloria, John, and Louis Renault all ended up in the delivery room with Rachel. John, feeling very out of place, tried to keep out of the way. All the nurses could do was lift Rachel onto the delivery table; by the time the doctor arrived and leaned over to take his first look, the child's head had already appeared.

When the infant's shoulders emerged, Rachel experienced a stab of such great pain that she cried out.

"John!"

Neither the doctor nor the nurses took much notice. After all, a birth that took less than three minutes was a kind of record for a first child.

"It's a girl!" the doctor declared, holding the infant up and administering two or three little slaps to her buttocks to get her wailing. The baby immediately complied, and a nurse handed the doctor a pair of scissors. The doctor turned to Louis, assuming he was the father, since he was wearing a tuxedo, and said, "Would the father like to cut the umbilical cord?"

Louis, who was basically a good-hearted fellow, began thinking fast, thinking about how his future wife had cried out for John in her most difficult moment of labor, a cry that came straight from her heart. He thought that if Rachel had really forgotten John she wouldn't have called John's name but his own instead.

And he suddenly realized that she'd never be happy with him, and that if he really loved her as much as he'd said he did so many times, he'd let her go, give her back to John. In any case, he wouldn't stand in the way of their reunion, even if it made him look ridiculous, even if he felt humiliated on what should have been his wedding day. After all, there were a lot more important things than pride or image, weren't there?

He looked at Rachel, who weakly smiled back at him, embarrassed because she was aware of what she'd uttered in her moment of distress, like a burning desire kept secret for too long. She knew she'd given herself away, and that she'd betrayed Louis, a good and honorable man.

But there was no hint of condemnation or reproach in Louis's eyes, only understanding and compassion, albeit tinged with sadness, just a touch of sadness, as a surge of love, a love that was greater than himself, rose up in his soul. Before Rachel said a word he'd already forgiven her.

He took the scissors from the doctor and held them out to John, who didn't understand at first. Why was Louis giving him the scissors?

Gloria understood immediately what the gesture meant, and turned to look at Louis. Was his heart breaking? She'd also heard Rachel cry out for John in her moment of pain, and knew just how much that cry must have hurt Louis as well, perhaps breaking something inside him forever.

But as she looked into Louis's eyes she didn't see the pain she'd expected, only regret. He regretted his folly in falling in love with a woman so young, young enough to be his daughter. He regretted having rejected Gloria's love, because now it was too late for her to bear children. He seemed to be asking her forgiveness, and gazing at her with his blue eyes, Louis saw that she understood what he was asking of her, that she forgave him and wanted him back.

"Here," said Louis, handing John the scissors. "Since you're the real father, you should do the honors."

John looked at Rachel and understood everything. He took the pair of scissors and cut the umbilical cord. The doctor, somewhat puzzled, made no attempt to understand this bunch of people. He took the baby, knotted the end of the cord skillfully, and then placed the infant in the arms of its radiant mother.

Gloria walked over to Louis and he took her hand, exchanging with her a look that confirmed their reconciliation. Louis then spoke the words that seemed to seal Rachel and John's destiny.

"Looks like this is the beginning of a very beautiful family."

POSTSCRIPT

In the four years that followed, John managed to sell two more screenplays, both of which were very successful in movie theaters across the country. Then, as one success led to another, he signed a contract for his next five screenplays, a contract that assured his status as a veritable millionaire.

For eight years, he and Rachel lived in peace raising their daughter, Gabriel, together. But then, suddenly, after all these happy years John was overcome with an irresistible desire to open the present the old millionaire had given him.